D0831050

All Things to All People

All Things to All People

The Catholic Church Confronts
the AIDS Crisis

Mark R. Kowalewski

State University of New York Press

Published by
State University of New York Press, Albany

For information, address State University of New York Press,
State University Plaza, Albany, N.Y., 12246

Production by Dana Foote
Marketing by Fran Keneston

Library of Congress Cataloging-in-Publication Data

Kowalewski, Mark R., 1957–
    All things to all people : the Catholic Church confronts the AIDS
crisis / Mark R. Kowalewski.
        p.   cm.
    Revision of thesis (Ph.D.) — University of Southern California
    Includes bibliographical references and index.
    ISBN 0–7914–1777–8 (alk. paper). — ISBN 0–7914–1778–6 (pbk. :
alk. paper)
    1. AIDS—(Disease) — Religious aspects — Catholic Church. 2. AIDS
(Disease) — Patients — Religious life. 3. Catholic Church.
Archdiocese of Los Angeles (Calif.) — History — 20th century. 4. Los
Angeles (Calif.) — Church history — 20th century. 5. California —
Church history — 20th century. 6. Catholic Church — Government.
I. Title.
BX2347.8.A52K683   1994
261.8'321969792—dc20   93–37730
                                                                    CIP

10 9 8 7 6 5 4 3 2 1

CONTENTS

PREFACE

Postmodern philosophical critiques of the notion of objectivity emphasize the importance of knowing the "subject position" from which discourse emerges. In this light, it is important to note my own perspectives in coming to this study. It is also necessary to locate this work within the context of my own experience.

Theologically, I am critical of assertions of hierarchical power in the Roman Catholic church over against the legitimate place of the laity to inform the church's moral discourse. The majority of the research and writing for this project was conducted while I was a practicing Roman Catholic layman. Yet this project represents in part my struggle with the Roman Catholic church. After I had written a draft of this book, and after a great deal of reflection, I left Roman Catholicism and was received as an Episcopalian. As I understand it, the vision of church that I discuss in the last chapter of this work exists more fully within the Anglican Communion at this moment in time. Nevertheless, the ecclesiology I advocate has been voiced by many women and men who have remained in the church. I could no longer stay. In this sense, my perspective is that of "protestant."

While this work is informed by my personal quest of faith, it is informed to no lesser a degree by my perspective as a sociologist of religion. This study is primarily concerned with how a normative organization deals with dissent in its ranks, and with a social problem that has the potential to compromise its views on sexual morality. As a sociologist of religion, I hold the perspective of objective observer as a necessary methodological construct. Yet this perspective is always partial for any social scientist. We will always see through the lens of our own lives. Thus, it is out of my dual subject position as a person of faith and a sociologist that I write this social analysis and critique of the response of the church to the AIDS crisis.

I must also acknowledge the people whose support, encouragement, and insights were invaluable in writing this book. Carol A. B. Warren's insights were a great help in the early stages of conceptualization. Donald E. Miller's responses throughout the writing of this work were always encouraging and challenging. It was under his direction that an earlier draft of this work appeared as my Ph.D. dissertation. The other members of my dissertation committee need to be acknowledged as well: Sheila Briggs, Jon Miller, and Charles Curran. I am very grateful for the support of a group of colleagues who met on a regular basis to discuss our work. They include Elizabeth A. Say, Robert J. Pierson, Freddele Spiegle, Lois Lorensen, and Bron Taylor. Brad Dusack and Peter Liuzzi who both served as director of the office for Pastoral Ministry to the Lesbian and Gay Community for the Archdiocese of Los Angeles were very helpful in providing information and contacts with priests. I thank the priests interviewed in this study for their time, interest, and insights. I also am very grateful for the constant support and encouragement provided to me by Steven Knise. Finally, I dedicate this work to Matthew Hirner, Mark Gifford, and all the thousands who have lost their lives in the fight against AIDS.

ACKNOWLEDGMENTS

The author gratefully acknowledges Monument Press for permission to reprint materials from Mark R. Kowalewski, "The AIDS Crisis: Legitimation of Homophobia or Catalyst for Change?" in *Homophobia and the Judeo-Christian Tradition*, ed. Michael L. Stemmeler and J. Michael Clark (Gay Men's Issues in Religious Studies series, vol. 1; Dallas, TX: Monument Press, 1990), pp. 147–63, and the Association for the Sociology of Religion for permission to reprint materials that originally appeared in article form in *Sociological Analysis: A Journal in the Sociology of Religion,* the official journal of the Association (1967–1992), vol. 51(1), pp. 91–94, 199x, and *Sociology of Religion: A Quarterly Review,* the official journal of the Association (1993–), vol. 54(2), pp. 207–17, 1993.

1

Introduction

This study concerns a normative organization's struggle to maintain stability while accommodating to the exigencies posed by a social problem. I will examine the response of the Roman Catholic church in the United States to the AIDS crisis, particularly as this disease has affected gay men. Gay people with AIDS (PWAs) present the church with a dilemma of status (Hughes 1945) in that they are simultaneously "sick" and "sinners" (Albert 1986). Church officials must respond in a manner consistent with the organization's "charter," that is, its official values and goals (Dingwall and Strong 1985).[1] On the one hand, Church leaders want to care for the sick, a traditional Christian ministry. In addition, they accept a scientific definition of AIDS as a viral disease, rather than a supernatural definition of the illness as a sign of God's wrath on a "sinful" lifestyle. On the other hand, the hierarchy wants to firmly maintain its traditional prohibition against homosexuality. To appear to accept homosexual relationships would represent an accommodation to social forces pressing for change, a compromise in what official church teaching maintains is divine law.[2] Such a compromise would threaten the hierarchy's authority in that it would give the appearance of yielding to pressure from interest groups within the church, as well as external forces. In hierarchical pronouncements, and through pastoral ministry to individual PWAs, the institutional church seeks to maintain organizational stability by steering a middle course in its response to AIDS and legitimating that response with reference to values mandated by its official charter.

This study, therefore, will examine the attitudes of American Catholic bishops who have made statements concerning the AIDS crisis, with particular attention to the bishops of California. I will examine bishops' attitudes on care for the sick, AIDS education, and discrimination against both PWAs and gay persons. I will also examine the attitudes and self-reported behavior of priests who have been involved in AIDS ministry or who expressed an interest in AIDS ministry. I will draw on interviews with priests from the Archdiocese of Los Angeles for this data.

For several reasons, my discussion will focus on statements on AIDS from the bishops of California, as well as the response to AIDS from the Archdiocese of Los Angeles. California has one of the highest rates of reported AIDS cases in the United States. The state also has two cities with large gay communities—San Francisco and Los Angeles. The Archdiocese of Los Angeles is an important focus, not only because it is the largest Roman Catholic archdiocese in the nation, but because it has experienced a great deal of controversy surrounding the church's proper role in the care of PWAs and in AIDS prevention. Finally, since Los Angeles has a large gay community, many priests there have had an opportunity to minister to gay PWAs. Thus, California, and the Archdiocese of Los Angeles in particular, provide a fertile setting for discussing the church's responses to AIDS and PWAs, particularly with regard to gay men.

No study on religion and AIDS to date has focused exclusively on the experiences and attitudes of priests or higher clergy. Seidler and Meyer (1989, 66) note the importance of focusing on priests and bishops when studying the Catholic church, since they are "pivotal figures" occupying key positions and performing key organizational functions. Fichter

(1968) notes that the opinions of priests are especially important because they are on the front line of pastoral care to
Catholic people on an everyday basis. Researchers have
focused on clergy responses to AIDS from various Protestant
denominations, however. Beckley and Chalfant (1988) studied the responses of Protestant parish clergy. While Bohne
(1986) included a small sample of priests in his study of hospital chaplains, he also dealt with clergy from several other
Christian denominations and did not deal with responses to
AIDS on a denominational level. The present study will deal
with the Catholic hierarchy and priests who minister in a
variety of contexts (parishes, hospitals, administrative posts,
etc.).

By focusing this study on the responses of the church to
gay PWAs, I do not intend to single out one social group as the
bearer of this disease. Indeed, anyone who has blood-to-
blood contact with any other individual carrying HIV can con-
tract the virus. However, this focus presents an opportunity for examining organizational "impression management"
(Goffman 1959) in the institutional church. Impression management is used to mediate the conflict between adherence to
traditional teachings and a desire to have relevance in the
modern world.

THE CHURCH AS A COMPLEX ORGANIZATION

This study examines the Roman Catholic church in the United
States as a complex normative organization (Etzioni 1961).
The Catholic church, like other institutional religious organizations, exists as an "open system" (Benson and Dorsett
1971; Scherer 1980), in that it is an organization constantly
responding to changes within its host environment. Various
elements within the church differ in regard to the proper
response to external social forces, alternatively embracing
the attitudes and behaviors of the larger society or denounc-

ing them (Harris 1969). Thus, forces both within the organization and outside it act as agents of institutional change. From this perspective, the church is seen as a "transformation process" (Scherer 1980).

Yet, as John Seidler (1986) maintains, organizational change within the church occurs as "contested accommodation." He states that the church has attempted rapprochement with the wider culture but also seeks to maintain social distance. While social forces pressure the church to change, other forces within the church resist accommodating to the host environment. It is conflict, Seidler argues, that initiates reform and compromise (see also Simmel 1955; Weber 1947, 132–35; Harris 1969; Foucault 1980b). Seidler mentions the shift toward democratic structures within the church as an example of institutional change. Priests and laity have gained a degree of organizational power through their participation in advisory groups such as priests' senates and parish councils. Yet countermodernizing forces in positions of power (e.g., the Vatican Curia) have resisted change, resulting in only a slight movement toward democratic structures within the church.

Seidler argues that change occurs in different segments of the church's structure and teaching at different times. While the inertia of the institution favors the status quo, the social environment, key events, or prophetic personalities, all may turn the tide in bringing about institutional reform. Seidler cites the Second Vatican Council as an example of a dramatic change brought on by a key event within the church.

Official Church teaching on sexual morality has certainly not been an area where change has occurred within the church, despite the changes initiated through Vatican II. Traditionalists, both clergymen and laypersons, uphold the traditional teaching of the church, as well as the hierarchy's claim to expert knowledge in moral matters. However, groups within the church have clamored for change in official teachings concerning issues such as birth control, abortion, and homosexuality. The AIDS crisis has the potential to act as a variable adding momentum to the forces of change in the American church's understanding of homosexuality or, alternatively, reinforcing the status quo. That is, there is a variety of positions the hierarchy may take to deal with the issue of homosexuality and gay men in the face of the AIDS epidemic. First, church leaders may see the Christian lives led by gay Catholic men, listen to their stories, and possibly be more open to a new understanding of homosexuality. A second possibility is that the hierarchy may see the disease as a reinforcement of a natural law theology that insists that homosexual activity results in disease because it is contrary to the natural purposes of sexual acts. Both of these positions have been advocated among church officials, as I will note in the following chapters. A third alternative is to allow limited accommodation in order to enhance organizational stability. I argue that this last alternative has chiefly characterized the response of church officials in the United States. In this case, accommodation represents an effort to rein in the forces of change and to keep modernizing elements under the control of the existing power elite.

In this regard, Philip Selznick (1948, 1966) notes that organizations attempt to maintain internal stability and continuity in policy and leadership in the face of external social forces that might threaten the organization. Selznick describes organizational behavior as motivated by a "prestige-survival motif" (Selznick 1948, 30). That is, organizational officials must not only try to survive in their social environments, but also save face and maintain social prestige. In other words, an organization must manage "multiple identities" (Cheney 1991) and convey a coherent image of the organization to both constituents and the environment. In short, it attempts to manage impressions both inside and outside the organization.

In his discussion of impression management, Erving Goffman (1959) notes that actors may perform as an impression management "team," with different actors taking various parts in order to achieve an overall effect. Pruitt and

Smith (1981) note a similar division of labor within organizations. They hold that organizational leadership must often remain firm when confronted with potential compromises. Firmness achieves two effects. It mitigates criticism from constituents who do not want organizational compromise, and it serves as a bargaining tool in negotiations with forces favoring accommodation, since firmness on the part of high-level management may help the other negotiating parties to accept less of a compromise than they originally desired. At the same time, the organization must appear trustworthy. It must show a willingness to collaborate with constituents seeking compromises (see also Magenau and Pruitt 1979).

One way to carry out this dual image of strength of position and willingness to dialogue is through a segmentation of personnel (Pruitt and Smith 1981). Higher-level officials wear "black hats," in that they maintain a hard line on organizational doctrine. Lower-level officials wear "white hats" and act as "conciliatory intermediaries." The organizational charter must be sufficiently vague about actions of lower-level officials in particular cases, so that effective informal negotiation may take place. In the present study, in most instances, the hierarchy wears "black hats" by publicly holding firm on church teaching, while priests wear "white hats" and negotiate the official teaching on the individual level.

Hierarchy in the Organization

In the Catholic church, bishops hold formal institutional power. Nevertheless, in the pluralistic American context, hierarchical authority rests on the "consent of the governed" (Scherer 1980). In the United States, churches exist as voluntary organizations. The Catholic hierarchy, therefore, can hold no authority if the Catholic people do not accept it and participate in the organization. Laity and even lower clergy, whose authority is derived from bishops, may exercise informal power within the organization through negotiation, or through participation in advisory groups, as noted above.

Yet this informal power is precarious (Kim 1980). As Winter (1968) states:

> Catholic organization can have an almost unlimited flexibility in the instrumentalities which it may use, so long as direction and control are in the hands of those to whom it was entrusted by the apostles. (108)

The hierarchy may, therefore, give a degree of autonomy to the laity, and to the lower clergy as well, but this power is ad hoc, informal, and contingent on the ultimate control of organizational structure and doctrine by higher administrative officials. It is the hierarchy that determines the organizational charter and thus determines what are "legitimate" organizational beliefs and actions. Formal authority within the institution is legitimated not by consent of the governed, but through the line of apostolic succession. That is, legitimate authority and church teaching can come through only those who succeed the apostles in leadership, namely, the pope, bishops, and priests as the bishops' representatives. In Weber's (1947) typology, the church fits a "traditional" legitimation of authority.[3]

Thus, the hierarchy attempts to maintain the stability of the organization, and its power within it, by allowing compromise and negotiation on the local level and by making use of normative means, such as traditional teaching, or the knowledge of "experts" both in theology and the natural and social sciences (Weber 1947; Vaillancourt 1980; Blau and Schoenherr 1971). However, it is important to note that such expert knowledge is selectively cited to reinforce and legitimate the hierarchy's teaching. In the present study, by maintaining a scientific understanding of AIDS and calling for ministry to the sick, those in the church hierarchy try to (1) maintain prestige in the host environment, (2) hold the allegiance of gay men, gay PWAs, and liberal Catholics who still retain church membership, and (3) attempt rapprochement with disaffiliated gays and gay PWAs. At the same time, they maintain continuity in policy and leadership by vigorously upholding both church teaching and their expertise as the only authoritative teachers in the church, thus solidifying their organizational power and maintaining their bond with conservative membership.

Priests in the Organization

I have noted that individuals in the hierarchy attempt to ensure the survival and prestige of the organization, as well as their power within it. Yet they also seek to maintain control over the lower clergy on the local level. The organizational authority of the priesthood is "franchised" to individual priests by the hierarchy, which has "proprietorship" (Maduro 1982) over priestly power. In discussing bureaucratic control within complex organizations, Blau and Schoenherr (1971) note:

> Power is rooted in the organization. No individual has it, and individuals merely make decisions through which this power is exercised as incumbents of positions in the formal structure. (352)

In the organization of the Catholic church, priests' professional identity is located not in themselves, nor in their professional expertise per se, but in the organization, which has the power to legitimate their ministry. At the same time, Blau and Schoenherr's point is overstated in that they leave little room for individual agency. Priests are not simply bearers of the official directives of the organization; they also exercise their ministry in the context of individual pastoral experience—an experience that often calls for compromise and negotiation.

Selznick (1966) notes that, in the face of pressure, delegated authority may often use discretion in carrying out organizational directives. Reynaud (1988), in his study of employee and management relations, states that employees negotiate between prescribed (*prescrit*) official directives and their actual (*reèl*) experience of the situations in which such directives must be carried out. Maduro (1982) discusses negotiation between, and within, two divisions existing within religious organizations.[4] The first is the division between laity and clergy, and the subordination of laity to clergy. The clergy have a monopoly on the control of religious production, and the laity seek to have their religious needs met. This is a potential source of conflict if the clergy will not extend their services to groups of the laity, or if the laity seek to appropriate the means of religious production themselves. Second, there is the internal division involving subordination of lower clergy to higher clergy. This situation may also result in conflict if the lower clergy attempt to gain a larger share in the power of religious production than they are allotted by the higher clergy, who attempt to maintain control. The interests of each of these groups need to be at least partially satisfied if the religious system is to maintain unity.

Priests attempt to remain faithful to hierarchical teaching and carry out their ministry to the sick, satisfying the interests of the higher clergy, yet make compromises to satisfy the interests of a group of laity whom they believe are dissatisfied and alienated. The freedom of negotiation priests experience in their pastoral ministry also helps to partially satisfy their desire to appropriate control over religious production. In the specific context of AIDS ministry, and perhaps in the Roman Catholic system generally, priests become mediating agents for the preservation of unity between higher clergy and laity, effecting compromises in the fulfillment of often disparate group interests and thus maintaining the relative stability of the organization.

Thus, the position of priests within the church is not simply that of "organization men" (Whyte 1956; Fichter 1974) who take orders from the hierarchy and apply them in their particular careers. In their study of priests' career satisfaction, Hall and Schneider (1973) note that the higher the level of autonomy priests experience, the more they feel challenged and successful in their careers. Indeed, lack of autonomy or "inner-directedness" is a major source of clergy disaffection and resignation (Schoenherr and Greeley 1974; Seidler 1979). Priests in the present study expressed autonomy through their ability to negotiate their interaction roles with PWAs as both pastors and official representatives of the church.

A priest's role as the church's official representative confines his actions in pastoral ministry. Yet his interaction roles with PWAs should not be understood as thoroughly scripted, or totally circumscribed by structural constraints. His actions are determined not only by organizational directives, but by his own inner-directedness, as well as by the role expectations placed on him by PWAs.

Callero (1986) states that an actor takes the role perspective of the larger community but expresses it through his or her individual perspective and experience. To carry out the theatrical metaphor commonly used in symbolic interactionism, an actor uses conventional roles (Shibutani 1961, Hewitt 1979) and improvises on them. In this study, priests use their inner-directedness to determine the extent to which they can compromise on hard-line church teaching in order to fulfill their conventional roles as pastor and counselor.

Coser (1979), in her study of resident psychiatrists in a mental hospital, noted the "structural ambivalence" (Merton and Barber 1976) inherent in the "dual mandate" under which residents dealt with patients. On the one hand, they used their authority to control patient behavior; on the other hand, they were involved in patient therapy—a relationship based on trust between patient and practitioner. This relationship is not unlike the negotiational situation noted earlier, where conflicting parties use the strategies of firmness and trust to achieve compromise.

In the present study, structural ambivalence also exists in the ministry of priests. They are called upon to uphold the magisterium's sexual teaching—a position of authority. At the same time they must minister to the sick, which often involves the counselor or therapist role—a position of trust. By proclaiming the views of the magisterium in public contexts while attempting to negotiate and compromise between PWAs and official church teaching in private contexts, priests work to mediate this ambivalence.

The Church in the World: The Quest for Stability and Relevance

I have noted the strategy of limited accommodation that the church has used to preserve its relevance or survival and prestige in the modern world. However, in the nineteenth century and continuing through much of the twentieth, the Roman Catholic hierarchy, particularly the papacy, sought other ways to protect the church from the social forces of the modern world, which threatened its stability from without. Such forces included the rise of democracy and pluralism and the increasing prestige of the natural and social sciences (Seidler 1986; Lyng and Kurtz 1985; McSweeney 1980; Vaillancourt 1980; Ellis 1969).

McSweeney (1980) notes three stages of hierarchical responses to modern Western society. The first stage lasted from the French Revolution until the death of Pius IX in 1878. During this period the hierarchy called for detachment from the modern world. The church was seen as a fortress, protected from the attacks of the modern age. The church's goal was to preserve the deposit of faith unscathed through the crises of modernity (see Dulles 1978). Since the church was thought to be under siege, dissent in the ranks would not be tolerated. It is important to note that in the United States during this period, Catholicism was largely a faith of European immigrants not yet assimilated into the American mainstream (Varacalli 1983). The ghetto mentality of the Vatican was therefore reflected in the life experience of the American church.

The second stage McSweeney discusses began with the pontificate of Leo XIII (1878) and lasted through the Second Vatican Council (1963–65). While continuing to remain antagonistic toward modernity, Leo advocated a policy of infiltration. Catholics, especially intellectuals, were called upon to understand secular views in order to bring a Catholic influence upon Western society. During this period, unrest from within also threatened the stability of the church. Catholic theologians and intellectuals increasingly believed that church teaching should be informed by advances in the sciences and saw the need to accept the religious pluralism and democracy of the modern West. Catholic intellectuals sought to make the church relevant to the modern world. At the same time, as Catholic laypeople entered the mainstream of American life and as ethnic ties began to lose their hold, democracy and religious pluralism became normative concepts for American Catholics.

The third stage, McSweeney notes, was brought about by Vatican II, initiated under the papacy of John XXIII. The council fathers, and the theologians with whom they consulted, sought to bring an end to the antagonism between the church and the world. As John XXIII noted, the church needed to open its windows to the world and begin a process of *aggiornamento*. In the post–Vatican II period, the church has adopted, at least in theory, a strategy of dialogue with secular society, addressing social problems and making use of the findings of the social and natural sciences in theological inquiry. This new strategy has been an attempt to increase the relevance of the church to a modern world. In advancing this strategy, church hierarchy seeks to preserve and enhance its prestige.

Seidler and Meyer (1989) understand Pope John's *aggiornamento* as the legitimation of a spirit of openness to democratic structures and pluralism within the church. The groundwork for this had been laid in the decades preceding the council both in the United States and in Europe. Seidler and Meyer also note that the council mobilized the forces for change. Additionally, in the years since the council the forces of change have sought to implement the modernization legitimated by the council. Yet, as I have noted above, this has been a contested accommodation.

Priests have also sought to advance the church's openness to the world. Many priests have entered other professions, while maintaining their status as priests, in order to enhance their ministry (see Fichter 1974). During the post–Vatican II period, the priesthood itself has increasingly been defined as a profession, not unlike the medical or legal professions, in which a particular expertise is gained and a service offered (Fichter 1974; Geany and Ring 1971; Fischer 1987). Such professionals, due to their expert training, maintain a degree of autonomy in professional decision making when dealing with "clients." In fact, Struzzo (1970) found that priests' image of themselves as professionals results in their dissent from church authority in conflict situations. Notions of autonomy and professionalization, while certainly present in the American church at least since the Second World War, have flowered in the post–Vatican II era.[5] As part of the professionalization of the ministry, priests have taken on new roles, such as those of administrator or therapist, in addition to the more traditional roles as sacramental functionary and pastor of souls.

The role of the laity has changed in the post–Vatican II church as well. One of the models of the church that emerged from Vatican II was that of the laity and clergy as "people of God" (see Dulles 1978). While this theological point existed in the church's theology before the council, it was certainly not emphasized. Rather, the clergy played all the official roles in the church with the laity standing by as spectators. In the postconciliar church, laity have assumed several ritual tasks once the domain only of priests. For example, laypersons read the Scriptures and distribute communion during mass. I have noted above, however, that the laity have received no real structural power. Yet laity have received more of a hearing from church officials than they previously had. In the "Pastoral Constitution on the church in the Modern World" (*Gaudium et Spes*), the laity are instructed to take up an active role in the church. The document states:

> Let it be recognized that all the faithful, clerical and lay,
> possess a lawful freedom of inquiry and of thought, and
> the freedom to express their minds humbly and coura-
> geously about matters in which they enjoy competence.
> (Abbott 1966, 270)

This openness to lay opinion, along with the council's view
that laity have a function or "apostolate" within the church,
has encouraged more Catholics to study theology. Indeed, as
Varacalli notes, a "new Catholic knowledge class" has
emerged as an interest group within the church in the years
following Vatican II. This segment of the church is made up
of educated, liberal laypersons who are theologically literate
and committed to carrying out the changes in the church
envisioned by the council as they see them. Changes these
Catholics envision include structural decentralization and
advocacy for the rights of the poor, the underprivileged, and
the disenfranchised, such as women and gays.

McSweeney (1980) notes the emergence of several
interest groups within the laity in the American church after
Vatican II; among these are Catholics seeking to make the
church politically relevant, inward-looking charismatic or
pentecostal Catholics, and traditional Catholics, whom I discuss below. Although not mentioned by McSweeney, gay
Catholics are another interest group within the church.
Especially in the United States, groups such as Dignity press
for acceptance of not only gay persons within the church,
but of monogamous gay unions as well. These varying factions vie for a voice in the church and are at times in conflict.

Despite the changes I have noted, the pre–Vatican II
intransigence of Roman Catholic teaching may hinder the
church's quest for legitimacy in the modern world (Kim 1980).
When an organization changes a position to which it has previously committed itself, it threatens the organization's legitimacy among its constituents (Pruitt and Smith 1981). Within
preconciliar Catholicism, as Gleason (1979) states, the majority of Catholics saw the church as theologically inviolable.

After Vatican II, it appeared to many Catholics that the whole structure of the church was called into question. In an effort to retain legitimacy in the eyes of traditional-minded Catholics, the hierarchy had to choose the middle course of opening the church to the modern world while still remaining faithful to traditional doctrines and holding on to established structures. As I have noted above, the church's response to the AIDS crisis is an example of its attempt to retain legitimacy among diverse constituencies as well as to appear relevant to the modern world.

THE LOCALIZATION OF POWER

Examining particular and localized expressions of power is necessary to an understanding of the whole structure of power within an institution. Therefore, I have based broader theoretical statements about the larger church organization on experiences of lower-level organizational officials, as well as on statements by upper-level officials with regard to one particular issue, the AIDS crisis.

Foucault (1980a) discusses the methodology of using local expressions of power to examine the structure as a whole. He states that structural power is expressed in localized and particular instances of discourse and that it is in these localizations of power that we can gain a perspective on the larger picture. Foucault discusses a method for analyzing relations of power. First, one must examine the "local centers" of power and knowledge. Foucault gives as an example the relation between penitent and confessor, where official knowledge is localized and power over the penitent is enforced. Second, Foucault notes that since power relations are not static, it is important to see how power is appropriated and transformed in its localizations. Third, he notes the importance of seeing how those individualized expressions fit into the "overall strategy." Inversely, the overall structure of the institution is supported by the local expressions of power. Fourth, Foucault notes that there are conflicting elements of discourse that act in tension even on the local level and these must be examined. He states:

> There is not, on the one side, a discourse of power, and opposite it, another discourse that runs counter to it. Discourses are tactical elements or blocks operating in the field of force relations; there can exist different and even contradictory discourses within the same strategy; they can, on the contrary circulate without changing their form from one strategy to another, opposing strategy. (Foucault 1980a, 101)

Thus, there are not simply two separate discourses, one emerging from the empowered and one from the powerless, but elements of both appear in expressions of discourse on the local level and even in the official discourse of those in power. It is these elements of discourse that help to bring about transformations of power. Foucault notes that these differing and sometimes conflicting elements must be objects of analysis as well.

My analysis utilizes Foucault's methodological cues for examining the power of institutions by looking at local centers of power within the hierarchical organization of Roman Catholicism. I also examine how relations of power are transformed on the local level, and how such transformations can serve the existing organizational power structure.

THEOLOGICAL CONSIDERATIONS

The organizational goals of preserving traditional teaching and allowing for pastoral accommodations are based in the Roman Catholic church's theological self-understanding. The church sees itself as interacting with society, not separated from it. In Troeltsch's (1981) sense, it represents the "church" type rather than the "sect." While eschewing the sinfulness found in the world, the church still affirms the goodness of the world and human culture and participates in it.

The church has within its membership both "saints" and "sinners." It takes a gradualist approach to conversion, unlike the sect, in that it accepts the fallibility of its members who have not yet reached Christian perfection. It is possible, then, in Catholic theology, to make pastoral accommodations in the objective teaching in order to achieve limited, imperfect good in an imperfect society and with an imperfect church membership.

Haring (1970, 140) addresses this gradualist approach when distinguishing between moral theology and pastoral counseling. As Haring states, "Pastoral prudence looks not only to the general principles, but also to the art of the possible." In this regard, Haring discusses the "law of growth," whereby one gradually comes to live out the church's objective moral teaching. A person who may not be able to live out objective moral teaching, he notes, is in a state of "invincible ignorance." This concept does not refer simply to an inability to understand the church's position on moral issues, but refers to all the real-world circumstances in which a person finds him- or herself and that impede the person from fully carrying out objective norms in her or his life.

Similarly, Curran (1984) notes that the pastoral minister is often confronted with the issue of dissent from church teaching in counseling situations. The pastoral minister, Curran writes, experiences the tension between authoritative church teaching and the conscience of the individual. The conscience should be formed by the gospel, and the Christian must live out the gospel's demands in "truth and practice." This commitment may lessen tension between the individual conscience and the church's teaching, but such a tension still appears in pastoral counseling situations. Curran states that while a "privileged place" must be given to the hierarchical magisterium, it is possible for a faithful Christian to dissent from it.

An important distinction needs to be made at this point. On the one hand, the Christian may see her- or himself as not reaching the ideal. In this sense she or he is growing in the faith, and pastoral accommodations may be made to compensate for human weakness. However, an individual may also dissent from the church's teaching on a particular point. He or she may have an ideal at variance with official teaching. Even in this case, Curran notes, the pastoral minister should respect the conscience of the individual.

The tension between the magisterium and pastoral practice also appears in papal teaching. In his hotly contested encyclical *On the Regulation of Birth* (*Humanae Vitae*), Paul VI strongly states his opposition to all forms of artificial birth control, but then focuses his attention on "pastoral directives." In addressing both married couples and priests, the pope emphasizes what Haring terms "the law of growth." Christ, the pope states, "was indeed intransigent with evil, but merciful toward individuals" (Paul VI 1968, 21).

The pontiff does not discuss those who dissent from church teaching. Rather, he confines his remarks to the issue of those who fall short of the ideal. A plurality of positions is not acceptable. In fact, priests are called upon to expound the teaching of the magisterium "without ambiguity."

John Paul II (1981) is also insistent on the need to maintain church teaching as the ideal. In his encyclical *On the Family* (*Familiaris Consortio*), he notes that even though pastoral practice should allow for gradual growth, church teaching itself is not negotiable. The pontiff asserts that married people are to follow the natural law as set forth in the official magisterium of the church. He notes that Christian love and forgiveness must nurture married people as they attempt to follow the church's teaching. Nevertheless, John Paul admonishes the faithful:

> [Married people] cannot, however, look on the law as merely an ideal to be achieved in the future: They must

consider it as a command of Christ the Lord to overcome difficulties with constancy. And so what is known as 'the law of gradualness' or step-by-step advance cannot be identified with 'gradualness of the law,' as if there were different degrees or forms of precept in God's law for different individuals and situations. (John Paul II 1981, 32–33)

In John Paul's theology, therefore, as in his predecessor's, there is little room for a plurality of moral positions.

While the possibility of dissent is not emphasized in papal teaching, respect for the well-formed individual conscience, as well as allowances for growth in conforming one's life to church teaching, is very much a part of the Catholic theological tradition.[6] This theological position gives freedom to the pastoral minister in counseling situations. It also allows for the church's organization to operate more effectively in the modern world.

AIDS: THE MEDICAL, SOCIAL, AND RELIGIOUS CONTEXT

The church's response to AIDS has not occurred in a vacuum. Rather, the church responds to upheavals in its host environment as well as from within its own ranks. Thus, it is important to discuss the disease itself and the ways in which the broader society has dealt with it as a social problem. I also will examine how other Christian communities in the United States have responded to AIDS. The diversity of these responses reflects the diversity of American Catholic responses to the AIDS crisis.

The History of AIDS in the United States: A Brief Note

In the spring of 1981, doctors at the UCLA Medical School discovered several cases of a rare form of pneumonia, *Pneu-*

mocystis carinii (PCP), occurring in young and otherwise healthy gay men. At approximately the same time, several cases of a rare cancer, Kaposi's sarcoma, were diagnosed in New York, again among young gay men. Both of these discoveries were reported to the Centers for Disease Control (CDC) in Atlanta.[7]

While more cases continued to appear among gay men, in the fall of 1981 other cases were found among heterosexual men and women whose common link was the use of intravenous drugs. A few months later, similar cases were found among Haitian immigrants. In early 1982, the CDC discovered that three hemophiliacs had contracted PCP.

In 1982 AIDS received its first name from the medical establishment, Gay Related Immune Deficiency (GRID)—a "homosexual stamp" firmly affixed to the disease (Liebowitch 1985, 3). Several of the early theories of the disorder linked it to gay lifestyle. Some researchers believed that the use of amyl nitrites, or "poppers," by gay men was linked to the disease. Others held that the sickness was the result of an overload on the immune system due to the high rate of sexually transmitted diseases among gay men. Still others postulated that the introduction of sperm into the bloodstream during anal intercourse accounted for the depletion of the immune system and thus susceptibility to the rare forms of infection that had been reported. These theories, however, could not account for the cases of the disease among drug users, Haitians, and hemophiliacs.

Eventually researchers began to believe that the disease was transmitted through blood products. They then began to propose the presence of a viral agent as the cause of the illness. These discoveries also brought about the renaming of the disease from GRID to Acquired Immune Deficiency Syndrome (AIDS).

Investigators endeavored to find the AIDS antigen as soon as a viral connection became clear. In 1984 a team of researchers in Paris headed by Dr. Luc Montaignier and another team in the United States under Dr. Robert Gallo isolated a new retrovirus in PWAs, which the American team called "HTLV-III." Since that time, however, the virus has generally been referred to as "Human Immunodeficiency Virus" (HIV).

After the discovery of the virus, a reliable test was developed to detect the presence of HIV antibodies: enzyme-linked immunosorbent assay (ELISA). Another confirmatory test, the Western Blot, was also developed.

Researchers found that the HIV virus is spread through three main routes of transmission (Friedland and Klien 1987). First, blood contamination may occur through sharing needles in intravenous drug use or through receiving contaminated blood products through a transfusion. However, the screening procedures available through HIV antibody testing have made the blood supply very safe. Second, sexual transmission of the disease may occur, primarily through anal or vaginal intercourse. The third route of transmission is from an infected mother passing on the virus to her unborn child perinatally.

Effective treatments to HIV disease have been elusive, and a cure or a vaccine is not likely to appear for several years. However, drugs such as zidovudine, or AZT, have proven to be temporarily very effective in treating the disease.

AIDS and American Society

The initial association of AIDS with gay men, and the fact that gays still make up the majority of the AIDS cases in the United States, have contributed to the popular understanding that AIDS is a gay male disease. Indeed, the terms *AIDS* and *homosexuals* have come to be synonymous (Altman 1987, 58). PWAs are often blamed for their disease, since it is assumed that they acquired it through "illicit, illegal or unacceptable sex" (Bennett 1987, 533). The gay community as a whole has been very generous in its care for PWAs and has been active in the political effort to gain increased local, state, and federal support for AIDS research and patient care. Yet the association between physical disease and an already stigmatized minority has hampered efforts of the gay community to gain social legitimacy (Altman 1987). The stigma of AIDS has caused some gay men to be ambivalent about their response toward PWAs (Kowalewski 1988).

The association between sickness and stigmatized behavior has fueled antigay political rhetoric (Bayer 1985; Brandt 1987; Altman 1987). For example, in California in 1986, political extremist Lyndon LaRouche sponsored an initiative on the California ballot (Proposition 64). LaRouche and his organization, the Prevent AIDS Now Initiative Committee (PANIC), produced literature stating that medical authorities have underestimated the threat of the disease to the larger society. PANIC also maintained that the virus could be contracted through casual contact. Measures such as quarantining of all carriers of the virus were said to be necessary to deal with AIDS as a public health threat. At the same time, the paper *New Solidarity*, tied to LaRouche's organization, stated that opposition to the LaRouche initiative came from "lower sexual classes" and "the degraded homosexual subculture so pervasive in California" (quoted in *Los Angeles Times*, 6 October 1986). LaRouche maintained that these extreme responses to AIDS were necessary public health recommendations. In reality, he manipulated the AIDS crisis to further his antigay political agenda. While Proposition 64 was not supported by any medical or political organization in the state, it still received enough signatures from California voters to easily qualify as a ballot initiative in 1986. A similar ballot initiative, Proposition 102, sponsored by Congressman William Dannemeyer of California, was defeated in 1988.

Since the disease was thought to affect socially marginalized groups and not mainstream American society, federal funding and medical efforts in AIDS research were slow in developing (Brandt 1987; Altman 1987; Patton 1986). Brandt states that another reason for a slow response in social policy to AIDS was a perception that PWAs bore the responsibility for their illness. Brandt (1987, 201) adds that such an approach moves away from a social policy protecting public health to one of punishment.

In a similar vein, discussion of public AIDS education has provoked a great deal of controversy. Public officials have questioned whether public educational materials, paid for with public funds, should include graphic discussions of safer-sex practices or discuss ways to avoid HIV infection while taking intravenous drugs. Officials have raised questions as to whether such discussion will promote "promiscuity" and drug use. Such questions are raised particularly in educational programs directed at youth.

At the same time, public health organizations have called for explicit AIDS educational materials directed at specific population groups. These organizations have advocated dissemination of safer-sex educational materials and condom distribution. They also advocate frank educational programs concerning sterile administration of intravenous drugs.

The care PWAs have received from medical professionals has been varied. Some health care providers have refused to give medical care to PWAs or have provided only minimal care. Altman (1987) notes that this response is motivated by both fear of the disease and homophobia. A survey of 314 Los Angeles physicians conducted in 1985 found that concerns about contagion deterred many physicians from treating PWAs (Richardson et al. 1987). Nevertheless, other health professionals have responded to the AIDS crisis by committing large amounts of time and energy to helping PWAs. As a result, burnout is a problem for many medical professionals who have worked extensively with PWAs (Morin and Batchelor 1984; Horejsi 1987).

Public health experts, government officials, and health care providers have responded in diverse ways to the AIDS crisis. While some have called for frank discussion of the methods of AIDS prevention, others have advocated discussion of only those means consonant with prevailing moral norms. Some have blamed the victims for the disease, but others have called for compassion and the expenditure of public resources to curb the spread of the epidemic.

A Review of Religious Responses to AIDS

Responses to AIDS from American religious communities have reflected, and in part shaped, the views of the broader society. I will review literature on AIDS from several Christian communities as a means of documenting the variety of responses.

One of the first articles to appear in the religious press came from the Moral Majority (Goodwin 1983, see also Falwell 1987), in which AIDS is defined as God's punishment on homosexuality—a position reiterated by other religious fundamentalists (see Altman 1987). Plantinga (1985), while not asserting that AIDS represents God's direct and active punishment of homosexuals, notes that AIDS is a logical outcome for those who violate the natural law. The notion that AIDS represents divine disapproval has been criticized by several writers (e.g., Krauthammer 1983; Altman 1986; Patton 1986; Shilts 1987). These commentators do not examine other religious responses to AIDS, however.

The majority of responses from the mainline Protestant religious press or from mainline denominations do not take the fundamentalist position. Yet few of these responses appeared in print until 1985 (see Beckley and Chalfant 1988). Hancock's (1985) discussion in *Christianity and Crisis* of compassionate treatment of PWAs and his call to eliminate irrational fears was one of the first articles to appear in a national religious publication. Several other articles calling for compassionate treatment of the sick as part of the church's ministry have appeared in mainline religious publications (e.g., Shelp and Sunderland 1985; Stone 1986; Nelson 1986; Boyens 1988). Some mainline publications have devoted whole issues to AIDS information and calls for AIDS ministry (see chapter 2). These articles do not deal with the

Christian prohibition against homosexuality. Vaux (1985) affirms a response of compassion for those stricken with AIDS, but also strongly maintains the traditional Christian prohibition against homosexuality. This distinction is clearly stated by evangelicals such as Frame (1985) and Sider (1988), who advocate that PWAs should accept traditional sexual morality.

More substantive treatments have also dealt with the need for AIDS ministry. Shelp, Sunderland, and Mansell (1986) report the stories of PWAs' struggle with their disease. Shelp and Sunderland (1987a, 1987b) maintain that PWAs are an oppressed minority who deserve the concern of the church. They also offer practical suggestions for churches wishing to become involved in AIDS ministry. They deal only briefly with the traditional prohibition on homosexuality, noting that care for the sick does not necessarily mean accepting homosexual relationships as normative. Fortunato (1987), however, affirms committed same-sex relationships as normative. His discussion of AIDS focuses on the spiritual relationship between PWAs and the suffering of Christ.

On a denominational level, the Episcopal General Convention (1985) endorsed a statement on AIDS calling for compassion for those affected by the disease and stressing the need for wider preventive education. The statement also repudiates the notion that AIDS represents divine punishment of gays. Several other denominations have taken a similar stance in either working papers, official position statements, or educational materials responding to the AIDS crisis (e.g., United Methodist Church 1986; Castro 1987; World Council of Churches of Christ 1987; National Council of Churches of Christ 1986; United Church of Christ 1987; Presbyterian Church U.S.A. 1988).

The Catholic press was also slow to deal with the issue of AIDS. Like the mainline Protestant responses, Woods (1985) notes the fear that has accompanied AIDS, and calls for Christian compassion toward PWAs. Nieckarz (1985) discusses his personal experience in AIDS ministry and questions the church's traditional condemnation of homosexuality. These articles have been reprinted in an issue of *Bondings* (1985–86) devoted to AIDS.[8] Another issue on AIDS appeared the following year (1986–87). The articles advocate compassion for the sick and discuss the church's response to PWAs. These writers generally dissent from the official church view on homosexuality. Gordon (1986) also is critical of the church's sexual teaching. He states that the church's care for PWAs has been too little and too late.

Other positions have been less critical of the official church. Flynn's (1985) work notes that the majority of PWAs have been gay men and questions the church's stand on homosexuality, exploring alternative perspectives from post–Vatican II moral theology. Yet she does not openly dissent from the church's position. An issue of *America* (1988) devoted to ministering to PWAs did not deal with the church's view on homosexuality, but focused on ministry to the sick. Other writers (e.g., Pawell 1986; Windsor 1987) have taken a similar position. In this regard, these responses are similar to those of mainline Protestant writers.

A minority of Catholic writers have taken a stance similar to fundamentalist Protestantism. Antonio (1986) states that AIDS represents the just deserts of violating God's law. He also advocates quarantining PWAs and presents erroneous medical information on AIDS (e.g., that the AIDS virus is spread by mosquito bites). Harvey (1987), while taking a more compassionate view toward the sick, also upholds the just-deserts position advocated by Antonio. A similar view is expressed in the conservative Catholic publication *Fidelity* (1987), of which an entire issue was devoted to questions of homosexuality and AIDS. The Vatican's Sacred Congregation for the Doctrine of Faith in its statement on homosexuality (1986) also alludes to this view in a reference to AIDS (sec. 9). Advocates of this perspective call gay PWAs to accept the church's teaching on homosexuality and repent of their lifestyle.

The Catholic hierarchy in the United States has generally taken a conciliatory stance in its discussion of AIDS. Among the earliest responses to AIDS from the hierarchy on an official level was the statement by the bishops of California (California Catholic Conference 1987), which advocated a Christian response of compassion toward the sick. The statement called for sensitive treatment of gay PWAs and also noted the needs of health care workers, women with AIDS, and PWAs in prisons. The administrative board of the United States Catholic Conference of Bishops issued a statement in 1987. Reiterating the church's call of compassion for sick persons, the bishops were also clear in their advocacy of the church's traditional teachings on sexuality. The statement was revised and later accepted by the bishops of the United States as reflecting their position on HIV. The response of the hierarchy to the AIDS crisis will be discussed in detail below.

While a minority of religious responses have simply seen AIDS as a divine punishment, the majority of responses from American religious groups have called for compassion for the sick. Yet many of these groups uphold the traditional condemnation of homosexuality and are faced with the dilemma of dual status presented by PWAs. Responses to this dilemma include upholding traditional morality on the general level while caring for the sick person on the particular level, or calling for conversion of PWAs as well as caring for them as sick persons. Alternatively, "gay affirming" (Bohne 1986) groups call the PWA not to repent, but to integrate his faith with his sexual orientation. This view is most often in opposition to official denominational positions on sexual morality. As I have noted above, Catholic responses to the dual status of PWAs reflect those of other Christian groups dealing with the AIDS crisis. Thus, when faced with a social problem that may compromise traditional teachings, religious communities steer a course between accommodating to the situation—in a quest for relevance—and retaining what they view as essential to the organization—in a quest for stability.

AIDS AND THE ARCHDIOCESE OF LOS ANGELES

The Archdiocese of Los Angeles was established in 1840 and became an archbishopric in 1936. The current borders of the archdiocese were formed in 1976 when Pope Paul VI established a separate diocese for Orange County. The Archdiocese of Los Angeles covers 8,762 miles and is the largest of the twelve ecclesial divisions in California. It covers all of Los Angeles, Ventura, and Santa Barbara counties.

The first official public response of the Archdiocese of Los Angeles to the AIDS crisis occurred in February 1986 when then Archbishop, now Cardinal, Roger Mahony celebrated a mass for PWAs at Blessed Sacrament Church in Hollywood. At that time the archbishop announced plans to open a hospice for PWAs. Mahony also called for compassion for those suffering from the disease and called for a rational medical response to the illness.

In October 1986, Mahony also appointed a priest in full-time ministry to PWAs and the gay community, Father Brad Dusak. In response to Mahony's call for AIDS ministry, Father Dusak sought support from priests in the archdiocese who were willing to serve PWAs should the need arise in their geographic area. Approximately 150 stated they were interested in such ministry; one-third of this number were bilingual. At the time data were collected for this study, Catholic priests made up the largest number of clergy from any denomination available for AIDS ministry referrals from AIDS Project Los Angeles. The archdiocese also organized day-long seminars on ministering to PWAs for priests who were interested in AIDS ministry. The sessions included general information on AIDS, as well as talks from PWAs themselves, family members, and other priests who already had gained experience in AIDS ministry.

In July 1986 Mahony was also one of the founding members of the AIDS Interfaith Council of Southern California, along with Bishop Robert Rusack of the Episcopal Diocese of Los Angeles[9] and Rabbi Allen Freehling, president of the board of Rabbis of Southern California. The council's purpose was

> to set the moral tone for the response to AIDS and to counter misinformation and fear about AIDS with education and compassion. (AIDS Interfaith Council 1986)

The group saw the defeat of California's Proposition 64 as an immediate goal for which to fight.

In December 1986, despite public endorsement of rational AIDS education and ministry to PWAs, the archdiocese abruptly ended its support of AIDS education programs targeted at the city's large Hispanic community. The proposed series of programs would have been conducted in Hispanic parishes throughout the archdiocese. Part of the preventive information to be discussed at the seminars, cosponsored by an AIDS service organization, AIDS Project Los Angeles, would have included information on condom use as a preventive measure against AIDS. After the first program, a local newspaper published the headline: "To Fight AIDS, Church Sanctions Condoms" (Los Angeles Herald Examiner, 6 December 1986). Dismayed at this misunderstanding, the archbishop stopped the programs the next day, stating:

> Knowledge of such medical methods is one thing. This, however, would be seen as a sanction for using condoms. We do not and cannot give such sanction. (*Los Angeles Times*, 7 December 1986)

The archbishop explained that such educational endeavors under church auspices might be understood as compromising church teaching. The image of the church's uncompromising stand on sexual morality took precedence over practical, pastoral education to prevent the spread of AIDS. A similar stand was taken by Mahony in 1987 in response to a pastoral letter issued by the administrative board of the United States Catholic Conference of Bishops. Mahony opposed the board's recommendation to allow for the discussion of safer-sex practices in church-sponsored AIDS education seminars.[10]

There have been masses for persons with AIDS across the archdiocese. On several occasions, Mahony has presided at these events. In April 1988, at another mass at Blessed Sacrament Church, Mahony publicly commissioned forty priests of the archdiocese to work with PWAs. Masses for PWAs have also included anointing of the sick, a sacrament that is believed to bring about spiritual, emotional, and even physical healing. The AIDS masses have drawn large numbers of gay people, especially representatives of Dignity. The Gay Men's Chorus of Los Angeles has provided music during several of these events.

The archdiocese has developed an AIDS awareness education team of adult volunteers who have undergone an AIDS education training program. They go to local parishes and Catholic high schools to speak to parents' groups, lay leaders, and adult education forums about AIDS awareness on the parish level. The archdiocese has also implemented the National Catholic Education Association's curriculum for AIDS education in Catholic schools. While information on condom use and safer-sex practices are not part of the curriculum, condom use is discussed if students raise the issue.

The archdiocese has been involved in care for PWAs through Catholic hospitals. Also, a residence for PWAs was opened in 1988 with the support of the archdiocese under the supervision of the Serra Ancillary Care Corporation in the Mid-Wilshire area of Los Angeles. Two other residences have opened as well. The residences were established to serve poor people with HIV disease who have no other resources.

Other components of the response to HIV within the archdiocese include a task force established to coordinate the various elements of ministry to PWAs, education, and residential care. Certain parishes have emerged as having a particular ministry to HIV-infected people. These parishes sponsor AIDS masses and provide support groups. One parish has sponsored a retreat for HIV-positive people.

PLAN OF THE STUDY

In this chapter, I have placed the American Catholic church's response to AIDS in the broader context of the institutional need for survival and prestige. I have also examined the history of AIDS in American society, as well as the responses to AIDS from various other Christian groups. In chapter 2 I deal with the methodology for the study, focusing primarily on interviews conducted with priests in the archdiocese of Los Angeles. Chapter 3 details the response of the hierarchy to AIDS. Chapters 4 and 5 examine the responses of priests to the AIDS crisis. Chapter 6 considers sociological implications of the study as well as implications of the church's approach to AIDS ministry. I conclude with a critical analysis of the church's response to AIDS as an effort to diminish criticism of the church and to bolster the authority of existing ecclesiastical structures.

2

Methods

Research for this study originally focused around some broadly defined research questions. How have religious institutions in the United States responded to the AIDS epidemic? How have religious institutions balanced their traditional prohibitions against homosexuality with their desire to care for the sick, since the majority of PWAs in the United States have been gay men? How has the AIDS epidemic influenced the reexamination of sexual ethics, particularly homosexuality?

While these questions gave direction to my initial inquiry, I did not begin with logico-deductive hypotheses that I set out to prove. Rather, the data for this study were collected and analyzed from a "grounded theory" perspective (Glaser and Strauss 1967; Charmaz 1981; Strauss and Corbin 1990). This process allowed me to produce theoretical constructs emergent in the data, rather than imposing a priori theoretical constraints on them. As Glaser and Strauss (1967) note:

> In discovering theory, one generates conceptual categories or their properties from evidence; then the evidence from which the category emerged is used to illustrate the concept. (23)

In this way a continuing dialogue exists between the data and the theory emerging from them. Nevertheless, the emerging analysis can then be placed within an existing theoretical framework. In this sense, grounded theory is grounded not simply in the data, but in theoretical "traditions" as well.

In an effort to answer these questions, and as an initial phase of research, I wrote to forty-two religious denominations requesting official position papers, working papers, or representative articles from religious periodicals. I received twenty-seven responses.[1] Six denominations either stated they had no position on the topic, responded with general information about the denomination, or held that denominational polity precluded one response for the whole denomination (e.g., they claimed to have a congregational church government).

While I sent letters requesting statements to a variety of religious organizations, the Bahais were the only non-Christian group to respond with a specific statement. Buddhists and Muslims replied but had no official response to AIDS. Since American culture has been shaped to a large extent by Judeo-Christian religious groups, I finally confined the search to Jewish and Christian responses. Since no Jewish group sent a response, and in order to expand the search of religious literature, I supplemented denominational documents with thirty-three issues of various religious periodicals published between 1985 and 1988, each of which contains at least one article on religion and AIDS.[2]

As a result of this search, I developed an exploratory typology of religious responses to AIDS (Kowalewski 1990). After examining the broad range of religious responses to the health crisis, I decided to narrow my research to groups that responded to the disease through some form of pastoral care for the sick. This eliminated many groups from the religious right that condemned AIDS as God's wrath on homosexuals and that did not expend resources on AIDS ministries. I also decided that the most effective way of gathering data and analyzing the role of religious institutions in responding to

AIDS was to localize my research and decided to examine a variety of religious congregations in the Los Angeles area that were ministering to PWAs. I designed a research project that would combine both ethnography of congregations ministering to PWAs and intensive interviews with both caregivers and PWAs.

Three difficulties hampered this research enterprise. First, most of the congregations in the Los Angeles area with a ministry to PWAs did not have enough clients at any time to allow consistent participant observation. Often ministry that did occur was not in a group context, but consisted of individual counseling—a setting in which ethnographic observation would have been intrusive even if agreed to by participants. Second, the low numbers of clients did not give me a large enough interview group. Third, it became apparent that any comparison of religious responses to AIDS would be difficult across denominational lines, due to varying theological traditions, church polity and structure, and so on.

Thus, I abandoned the first design and focused exclusively on one religious tradition, Roman Catholicism. Methodologically, Roman Catholic responses to AIDS were analyzed for two reasons. First, the Catholic church has been very vocal in its response to AIDS. Being in Los Angeles, the largest Catholic archdiocese in the United States and one that has made an important effort at AIDS ministry, gave me a rich source of data from which to draw. Second, since I was a Roman Catholic at that time, my own personal perspective brought me to examine Catholic responses to AIDS as well. My research focus included public statements on AIDS made primarily by the church hierarchy as well as interviews with priests. Statements by bishops on the AIDS crisis are important in that they represent the official stance the American church takes toward the issue of AIDS ministry. Also, while laypeople and religious sisters and brothers represent the church by caring for the sick and conducting limited spiritual ministry, priests are the church's official representatives in pastoral settings. Thus, priests became the population I chose to interview. This population also allowed me to look at the broader issue of how the official church dealt with pastoral situations.

Interviews with PWAs would have been helpful in understanding the encounters priests had with PWAs, but priests noted that they often saw PWAs only on one or two occasions and did not have ongoing relationships with many of them. Also, in most cases, the PWAs to whom priests had ministered had already died. Priests were understandably very protective about the identity of PWAs with whom they were in contact, and only a few priests currently were seeing PWAs on a regular basis. These factors made it very difficult to conduct interviews with a sample of PWAs to whom priests ministered.

❦

DATA COLLECTION AND ANALYSIS

❦

Comparing themes from interviews with priests as well as the broader perspective gained from official statements made by church hierarchy brought to light some larger analytical issues. It became clear that the church's response to the AIDS crisis could be examined in light of the institutional issues of power, legitimation, prestige, and organizational impression management, as discussed in chapter 1. In light of these analytic findings, the church's response to the AIDS crisis became the case study for a broader analysis of the church as a normative and hierarchical organization.

Documents as Data

A large body of documents (noted above) was garnered to examine how religious groups responded to AIDS. When the locus of research became more precise (i.e., Roman Catholic responses to AIDS), I examined Catholic periodicals. I realized that documents written by bishops would provide a rich source of data on the views of higher-level clergy in the organization. Using official documents was especially useful for examining the attitudes of bishops, because their primary role in the church is that of policymaking for the organization. Their power is, of course, limited by the Vatican and the pope—the ultimate policymaker in the organization. Bishops' positions on AIDS, especially in official pastoral letters, present the official policy they wish to publicly set forth. Such statements not only serve to guide constituents and lower-level officials, but also provide a vehicle for publicizing the official stance on social problems to the broader society outside the organization.

Using documents as data also allowed me to triangulate (Denzin 1970; Fielding and Fielding 1986) the modes of observation used for the study. Analyzing documents provides a mode of "passive observation without social interaction," while interviews allow for "active observation with social interaction" (Rossi 1988).

Additionally, a third type of data helped inform my perspective but does not appear explicitly in this study. I attended ten masses for persons with AIDS held at different churches in the archdiocese. Cardinal Mahony presided at two of these, and Bishop Arzube presided at one. While I took field notes from these events, these data were primarily background for my main data sources of episcopal documents and interviews with priests. These ritual events allowed for participant observation of clergy "at work," ministering to PWAs in a public context.

Generally, the sermons at these liturgies focused on the church's mission to show compassion toward the sick and on the healing power of Christ. The masses also incorporated an anointing ceremony at which PWAs and those affected by the disease in any way were invited to come forward to receive anointing with oil and prayers for emotional, psychological, spiritual, and even physical healing. Thus, the role of PWAs as sick persons was emphasized in the context of the AIDS liturgies I attended.

The relationship between AIDS and homosexuality was often implicitly dealt with at AIDS masses, but not generally dealt with explicitly. At two of these liturgies, music was provided by the Gay Men's Chorus of Los Angeles, and members of Dignity[3] often served as lectors. Gay men also made up a large portion of the congregation. Bishop Arzube directly addressed the issue of gay men in the church during his sermon. He noted that it was possible to dissent in conscience from church teaching. This was the most open discussion of the issue of homosexuality at any of the AIDS liturgies I attended.[4]

Interviews with Los Angeles Priests

A total of thirty-two priests were interviewed for this study during the fall and winter of 1987–88. An initial list of priests interested in ministry to PWAs was provided by the archdiocesan director for ministry to the gay and lesbian community, who was also the director of AIDS ministry, Rev. Brad Dusak. I began with a group of twenty-five names drawn from the list of 250 priests in the archdiocese who wished to be contacted for ministry to PWAs (see chapter 1). The list of names reflected those priests whom Fr. Dusak knew personally and believed would be willing to discuss AIDS ministry. I interviewed twenty-three priests from this list.

The remaining nine interviews were gained by a "snowball" data collection method (Biernacki and Waldorf 1981). Interestingly, several of the priests I interviewed recommended names already on the list I had been given initially. This fact highlights Biernacki and Waldorf's observation that the snowball or "chain referral" method allows for tapping natural interaction networks. I gained consent for interviews, as well as established rapport with respondents, by mentioning that fellow priests, who were also friends, had referred me to them. While the interview data do reflect a wide array of responses, the sampling of interaction networks may not reveal variations in the population, as Biernacki and Waldorf caution. For example, no respondent saw AIDS as a divine punishment on gays. While such a belief may exist in the wider population of priests in the archdiocese, it is not reflected in my sample; nor did priests believe this attitude was prevalent in the priests they knew. Thus, while the attitudes and behaviors reported in this study are likely to reflect the views of priests who are open to AIDS ministry, they may not reflect the larger community of priests in Los Angeles who are outside the network of priests I interviewed or who did not volunteer to minister to PWAs.

Interviews with priests were semistructured. A list of twenty questions was asked of all priests during the course of the interview, but other questions were asked for clarification or to tease out an idea brought up in response to the standardized questions. Responses were open-ended, and respondents were encouraged to speak as long as they liked on an issue. At the end of the interview, respondents were asked to comment on any other aspect of their individual response to AIDS, the church's response, or the issue of AIDS in general that was not covered during the course of the interview. Interviews lasted between one and one and one-half hours. They were generally conducted in the parish rectory or in the priest's office. Interviews were tape-recorded (see Briggs 1986, 99) and later transcribed.

A Profile of Priests in the Sample

A wide range of ages is reflected in the sample; the youngest priest was in his mid twenties, the oldest in his late sixties. The median age of respondents was forty-four. Education was generally constant, with all sample members having at least a college and seminary degree. As Wolf (1987) notes, variables that might fluctuate with other populations—sex, marital status, and religion—are constant with a sample of Roman Catholic priests. A slight majority of respondents (seventeen) were parish priests; seven others were involved in various other ministries (e.g., campus ministry, full-time counseling); three worked in administrative positions; three were hospital chaplains; and two were teachers. A total of twenty-four priests had already engaged in ministry to PWAs at least once, through either ministry to the gay community (e.g., through Dignity), hospital chaplaincy, contact with family members who were parishioners, or, rarely, ministry to PWAs who were parishioners themselves. Two priests noted that they knew gay men with AIDS but did not minister to them as priests. Six priests had never ministered to a PWA.

Only two priests mentioned having ministered to a PWA who was not gay. No priests mentioned that the sexual orientation of the PWA would impede their ministry to the sick. Yet, in determining respondents' attitudes toward homosexuality, it was helpful to employ the categories Bohne (1986) uses in his study of hospital chaplains. He states that chaplains were either "gay condemning," citing antigay biblical passages or advising PWAs to get medical treatment for homosexuality; "gay neutral," in that they upheld traditional prohibitions against homosexuality but tried to distinguish between the PWA and acts that were objectively "sinful";[5] or "gay affirming," in that respondents did not regard homosexuality as pathological.

In the present study, no priests were gay-condemning, eight were gay-neutral, and twenty-two were gay-affirming. I use *gay-affirming* to refer to those priests who at least accepted monogamous same-sex relationships as morally acceptable for constitutionally gay persons. In this respect they dissented from official church teaching. Many of these priests saw such unions as inferior to heterosexuality, which they understood as the moral norm, but pastorally permissible because of the sexual orientation of gay persons. Other priests saw monogamous gay relationships as the moral equivalent to heterosexual marriage. The high number of gay-affirming priests in my study group is a product of both the nature of the snowball sampling technique and the perspective of priests attracted to AIDS ministry. Priests who volunteer for this work realize that they will be ministering to gay persons and are generally more open to ministering to gays. Volunteering for AIDS ministry often came from priests' prior pastoral experience with Dignity members.

Interviewing Methodology: A Further Note

In ethnographic research, participant observation is often considered the most complete way of getting at a social reality, as Becker and Geer (1957) note. Interviewing about social interaction is certainly not as complete a picture as observing the interaction and talking to participants about what the interaction means. Yet, as Trow (1957) has commented, the choice of tools a researcher uses depends on what she or he wants to create.

In studying the church's response to the AIDS crisis, I was not simply interested in the dyadic encounter between the priest and the individual PWA, although this is an important component of the church's response to AIDS. Rather, I sought to examine ministry to PWAs within the larger context of the church's response to AIDS. Interviews with a variety of priests gave me a wider range of responses than would a concentrated look at the work of only a few priests.

Briggs (1986) sounds a further note of caution with regard to interviews. The interviewer, he states, does not serve simply as a conduit for the views of respondents. Each interview must be seen as a social event where both partners are coparticipants in constructing the discourse. Thus, the researcher attempts to articulate the social world as he or she sees it, or as it is described by respondents, but such articulation is always filtered through the researcher's values and the experiences she or he brings to data collection and analysis.

In an effort to mitigate these research problems, Briggs notes the importance of making every effort to make sure questions mean the same thing to both parties in the interview. This requires the researcher to gain a knowledge of the language of respondents. Cicourel (1982) also notes the importance of having open-ended questions in the interview setting to allow for the respondent to explain his or her perspective more fully and to reduce constructions imposed on the data by researchers. My background in the "language" of Roman Catholic theology and knowledge of the culture of Roman Catholicism as an "insider" (although I am now an "outsider") allowed me to articulate interview questions in a way that respondents could easily understand. Conducting interviews on priests' turf, as well as giving priests the opportunity to discuss issues in an open-ended fashion within a limited structure, helped to reduce, but certainly not eliminate, potential problems of researcher interference.

MODELS OF THE CHURCH

I examine the church as a complex normative organization sociologically similar to other complex organizations. Much of the analysis in this study is grounded in social theory rather than theological ideals. Yet theologians contend that the church is essentially a spiritual reality eluding social-scientific investigation. Gustafson (1961) raises some questions in this regard:

> How can the same phenomenon, the church, be understood from two radically diverse perspectives? Does the use of doctrinal language require inherently the exclusion of the language of social thought? Does a social interpretation of the church necessarily exclude the more distinctively theological and doctrinal interpretation? If the two are not mutually exclusive, how can the significance of the social processes and elements be theologically understood? (100)

These questions are necessary to raise concerning my discussion of the church as a complex organization. Focusing too narrowly on a theological perspective masks the reality of existing power relations within the organization. The social-scientific point of view contributes to theological discourse by shedding a critical light on current church structures.

McKenzie (1966, 138) critiques the use of the sociological perspective as it applies to the church, stating: "The church has an organization; it is not an organization. The church is the body of Christ in which the Spirit dwells." McKenzie further asserts: "The mysterious reality is not grasped by reason, but accepted by faith" (177). He rejects attempts to understand the church through rational analysis of the organization.

Bartholomew (1981), commenting on McKenzie, notes that examining the church under any sociological model results in reductionism for McKenzie. Bartholomew compares the Jesuit theologian's approach with that of Gustafson (1961), who notes that sociological investigation of the church's institutional and social character can be useful in gaining a deeper understanding of the church. Yet, Bartholomew concedes, the sociologist cannot "solve the concern of a position like McKenzie's which insists on the essential quality of mystery in the authority of the church" (McKenzie 1966, 122).

Nevertheless, while the sociologist can be accused of scientific reductionism if he or she examines the church as "nothing but" a complex organization, a theologian such as McKenzie is guilty of "theological reductionism" (Gustafson 1961) or, better, theological obfuscation. Asking critical sociological questions does not deny the elements of mystery in the church perceived through the eyes of faith. McKenzie asks only the normative question: What should church authority look like? Yet descriptive and critical sociological analysis examines the ways in which the church's authority and power structure exist in the present moment, which then allows for critical theological reflection. Asking only the normative questions short-circuits critique based on an analysis of social power and social structures.

Thus, the sociological angle of vision presents one model of the church, a valuable perspective among many other more theological models, such as those Dulles (1978) presents. All models of the church express aspects of the ecclesial reality. Each model has its drawbacks, but, more importantly, each highlights certain elements for examination. No one model can claim to have a view from all sides. A richer understanding of the church requires a plurality of perspectives, including not only the theological, but the social-scientific as well.

3

The Hierarchy Responds to AIDS

Organizational officials inevitably seek to enhance prestige and ensure the survival of the organization, as I have noted above. Officials desire to maintain continuity in structure and doctrine within the organization and yet appear relevant to the modern world. In responding to the AIDS crisis, the Roman Catholic hierarchy attempts to maintain survival and prestige by steering a middle course between accommodating to the needs of those affected by AIDS and remaining firm in their prohibition against homosexuality.

The dual goal of caring for the sick and upholding organizational positions corresponds to the hierarchy's roles, respectively, as pastors and official teachers. Since the objective teaching of the church needs to be applied on the pastoral level, these two roles often conflict. I have noted that one way to resolve such conflicts is through segmentation of personnel (i.e., bishops as teachers and priests as pastors). Yet the hierarchy itself advocates, in its discussions of AIDS and homosexuality, both care for the sick and condemnation of homosexual acts. The hierarchy mediates the potential conflict between these positions through "attention deployment" (Sarbin and Allen 1968), whereby actors direct attention away from one of the conflicting roles through role compartmentalization. Burchard (1954) discusses this type of resolution in his study of military chaplains. In his sample, chaplains saw themselves as officers when they performed military duties and as chaplains when they performed religious duties. In addressing the AIDS crisis, the Catholic hierarchy also deflects attention from one role by focusing on another. When considering AIDS as embodied in sick persons, the hierarchy takes a conciliatory stand. Yet when discussing AIDS prevention, not embodied in PWAs, the hierarchy remains firm in upholding traditional sexual morality. Thus, in the former context the hierarchy acts as pastors and in the latter as teachers of the magisterium.

In advancing their dual position of firmness and conciliation, church authorities must convince their audience of the correctness of their position. As Goffman (1959, 204) notes, "Power of any kind must be clothed in effective means of displaying it." Organizational officials use expert opinion, as well as their position in the hierarchy, as bases of their authority (French and Raven 1959). In their discussion of impression management, Richardson and Cialdini (1981) note that one's public image is raised or lowered depending on the positivity or negativity of the things or persons with which one is associated (see also Tedeschi and Reiss 1981). An actor tries to convey a positive image of legitimacy and prestige by "basking in reflected glory" or, alternatively, "blasting" or denigrating things or persons having a negative association. Roman Catholic organizational officials, who constitute the hierarchy, attempt to associate themselves with rational, scientific responses to AIDS. Indeed, medical language is used to corroborate traditional teachings. In this way individuals in the hierarchy bask in the prestige of medical and scientific authority, as well as their own religious expertise as official teachers; and in this way, they attempt to legitimate their position to more traditional Catholics, as well as liberal Catholics and the wider audience of all "people of goodwill" (United States Catholic Conference of Bishops Administrative Board 1987).

Religious organizations also persuade their audience of their positions by supporting their arguments with in-group rhetoric. Religious rhetors assume a degree of common ground with their audience, other members of the organization, by rooting their argument in the religious tradition (Hart 1973). The hierarchy roots its discussion of AIDS in the rhetoric of the organizational charter and attempts to hold conservative support by firmly upholding traditional teaching. The American hierarchy in particular attempts to persuade these constituents of the need for a compassionate response toward PWAs who are sick and suffering individuals. Both care for the sick and adherence to the magisterium are firmly rooted in organizational tradition. At the same time, by maintaining a response of compassion toward the sick and reconciliation of alienated individuals on the pastoral level, which is also part of the organizational charter, the hierarchy attempts to win the support of alienated gays and liberal Catholics, and perhaps persuade them of a more conservative stance with regard to the official teaching of the church.

THE VATICAN AND AIDS

Since the Roman Catholic church is a hierarchical institution, it is necessary to discuss statements on AIDS made by top officials—the pope and the Vatican—before turning the discussion toward the American hierarchy. While the Vatican has not made an official statement on AIDS, it has made an indirect reference to AIDS in a statement on homosexuality, which states in part:

> Even when the practice of homosexuality may seriously threaten the lives and wellbeing of a large number of people, its advocates remain undeterred and refuse to consider the magnitude of the risks involved. (Sacred Congregation for the Doctrine of the Faith 1986, sec. 9)

From this perspective, homosexual acts in themselves, rather than the AIDS virus, are responsible for the spread of AIDS. The Vatican uses this dubious medical legitimation to promote its moral position.[1] The letter further implies that, in the interest of public health, the church cannot endorse laws protecting the civil rights of homosexuals, since it understands homosexual acts as life threatening.

The letter condemns violence against homosexuals, yet warns that when governments enact gay rights laws, violent reactions should not be surprising (sec. 10). In this view, both AIDS and violent reactions toward gays are examples of the societal chaos that ensues when individuals or societies violate the natural law (cf. Berger and Luckman 1967, 39). AIDS and antigay violence are both held up as the natural outcome of violating allegedly immutable moral norms.

While Vatican officials attempt to gain a medical endorsement for their negative views of homosexuality, they also denigrate those who advocate gay rights. The letter states that since homosexuality is a public health threat, those who advocate rights and freedom for homosexuals are refusing to stop the spread of AIDS. "The church can never be so callous" (sec.9), the Vatican asserts. By adhering to the traditional prohibition against homosexuality, church officials state, they are helping to stop the spread of AIDS, while gay rights advocates only hinder the church's efforts. Thus, the Vatican letter reverses the critique advanced by gay activists—that the church is doing little to stop AIDS because of its homophobic views—by stating that gays themselves stand in the way of bringing the AIDS crisis to an end.

Beyond seeing homosexuality as physically dangerous, the Vatican uses psychological language in defining homosexuality itself as a disease. The letter states that, while homosexuals should receive the respect and dignity due all human persons, they are intrinsically disordered and dysfunctional. While homosexual persons are worthy of pastoral care and counseling because of their "disorder," the question of the morality of gay sexual relationships remains unexamined, since the immorality of such actions is assumed a priori in the church's "constant tradition" (sec. 7). The Vatican condemnation of homosexuality is clothed in a psychological as well as a theological legitimation.

The Vatican letter upholds traditional antigay positions with a traditional legitimation—that moral teaching is unchanging and is safeguarded by church leaders—as well as a pseudomedical and rational legitimation, that abstaining from homosexual sex is a health precaution. At the same time, the letter advocates pastoral care for homosexual persons on a pastoral level. Yet the goal of this care is to convince homosexual persons of the authority of the hierarchy's teaching and to help homosexuals cope with their "dysfunctional" sexual orientation. From this perspective, if gays and PWAs are to be reconciled with the church, there can be no compromise in the church's teaching.

Furthermore, in a statement issued to the bishops of the United States (Sacred Congregation for the Doctrine of the Faith 1992), the Vatican attempted to clarify the position it advocated toward homosexuals in the 1986 letter. Given the belief that homosexual persons are dysfunctional, the 1992 statement asserts that the rights of homosexuals in civil society may be abrogated. The statement goes on to compare the legitimacy of restricting homosexual rights with restrictions placed on the mentally ill "in order to protect the common good."[2]

Pope John Paul II gave a more conciliatory impression in his remarks to PWAs at Mission Dolores Basilica in San Francisco in September 1987. The pope emphasized the church's care for all those who are ill and noted that God's love is embodied in the church. The pope went on to say:

God loves all without distinction and without limit . . .
He loves those of you who are sick, those suffering from AIDS and AIDS-related complex. (*The church World* 8 October 1987, 8)

While the pope concentrated on God's love and acceptance, he began his address by noting that God's love calls all people to repentance of sin and conversion. Though stated in very general terms, the pope's message was certainly intended to call gay PWAs to repent of their lifestyle. Also, when speaking of God's love and acceptance, the pope focused on PWAs' identity as sick persons and not as gay persons. While the pope invited PWAs to reconciliation with the church, giving the impression of openness, he did so on the church's terms. From John Paul's perspective, God's love is mediated through the church and thus through the church's authority. Reconciliation comes through accepting the church's teaching as articulated by the pope and bishops. The pope's emphasis on care for PWAs is an extension of the Vatican's attitude about caring for homosexuals as psychologically dysfunctional. That is, the hierarchy opens its arms to reconcile the sick, but on its terms.

THE AMERICAN BISHOPS AND AIDS

The American bishops have advocated pastoral care and temporal assistance for the sick and have spoken out for the civil rights of PWAs. At the same time, they have emphatically upheld church teaching regarding sexual morality. While my focus is on the pastoral pronouncements of Catholic bishops in California, the themes expressed are similar to those of other U.S. bishops who have made statements regarding the AIDS crisis.[3] I also discuss two pastoral letters, one from the administrative board of the United States Catholic Conference of Bishops (USCCB), written in 1987, and one adopted by all the bishops in the United States in 1989.

A Call to Compassion

A theme that appears frequently in pastoral letters written by bishops in the United States is that of understanding AIDS

as a disease contracted through very specific routes of transmission. Bishop Francis Quinn of Sacramento (F. Quinn
1986), for example, goes into detail concerning the ways
AIDS is transmitted. Further, the California bishops have
called for an end to discrimination against PWAs and uphold
compassion for the sick as a Christian duty. The bishops
reject attempts to blame PWAs for their disease. In a pastoral
letter on AIDS, "A Call to Compassion," the bishops affirm
that "AIDS must never be considered a divine punishment
for a person's sexual orientation, life-style or sexual activity"
(California Catholic Conference 1987, 3).[4] Archbishop John
R. Quinn of San Francisco further elaborates this point by
specifically defining the Catholic response to AIDS in opposition to fundamentalist Protestants, stating that Catholics

> should be guided by the church, which teaches in the
> Introduction to the Rite of Anointing and Care of the Sick
> that "sickness, while it is closely related to man's sinful
> condition, cannot be considered a punishment that man
> suffers for his personal sins." (J. Quinn 1986, 504)

The archbishop defines AIDS as a medical condition demand-
ing a rational response from society; it is not an indication of
God's wrath.

This view is spelled out more clearly in a public policy
statement the California bishops issued based on "A Call to
Compassion." The bishops call for care for those afflicted
with the disease. They state:

> People with AIDS/ARC remind us that they are not dis-
> tant unfamiliar victims to be pitied or shunned, but per-
> sons who deserve to remain within our communal con-
> sciousness and to be embraced with unconditional love.
> (California Catholic Conference 1988, 789)

In advocating this response, the bishops note the example of
Jesus, who reached out to all who were sick. The California

bishops echo Bishop Francis Quinn, who calls for an end to
the fear and ignorance about AIDS, stating:

> It [the AIDS epidemic] is, above all, a time for us to be
> true Christians and to be church, as the body of Christ,
> always solicitous for its wounded members. (F. Quinn
> 1986, 225)

The bishop also calls for Catholic hospitals and Catholics in
general to care for PWAs. Additionally, he discusses the pastoral role of the church toward PWAs:

> As church we can offer a healing ministry of reconcilia-
> tion to help restore a sense of wholeness to broken rela-
> tionships between the patient, family and friends. All
> responsible for administration of the sacraments shall
> be especially sensitive to the particular needs of people
> with AIDS. (225)

While the bishop notes the importance of both practical
assistance to PWAs and spiritual support, he does not
address the broken relationship that may exist between the
PWA and the church, or the church's official teaching on sexuality, which often has been a source of the alienation experienced by the PWA. Rather, there is a separation between
church teaching on sexuality and the treatment of PWAs.

The California bishops, in their pastoral letter, observe
that AIDS has affected both heterosexual men and women,
but that gay men have made up the highest number of AIDS
cases. The bishops' conciliatory stance is extended to
include not only gay PWAs, but gay people in general. In one
paragraph devoted to "special concerns for homosexual persons," the bishops state:

> The most obvious high risk individuals will continue to
> be members of the homosexual community, some of
> whom have been separated from the church and its

spiritual life. We regret this distance, and long to heal their wounds by offering our support and fellowship. (California Catholic Conference 1987, 789)

Whether this statement is a movement toward a dialogue on the church's moral teaching remains unclear. Yet the tone of this passage is conciliatory toward the gay community and holds out the hope of reconciling those who feel alienated from the church.

Nevertheless, the bishops uphold the church's teaching in an earlier paragraph where they state:

Avoidance of illicit use of drugs, sexual abstinence before marriage and monogamous fidelity within marriage recommend themselves as medically necessary as well as morally responsible. The recovery of the virtue of chastity may be one of the most urgent needs of contemporary society. (788)

While monogamy of any kind, with or without marriage, would help to curb the spread of the virus, the bishops tailor the medical facts to conform with their moral position by maintaining that "marital monogamy" is medically as well as morally wise.

Thus, the California bishops not only give a medical definition of AIDS, in opposition to less enlightened religious responses, but they also call for compassionate treatment of PWAs and reconciliation of gay persons with the church. At the same time, the bishops uphold church teaching on sexual issues but do not discuss what impact this teaching has on their call for a dialogue with the gay community and pastoral ministry to PWAs.

The Many Faces of AIDS

Like the California bishops, a body of national bishops has noted the many different groups at risk for contracting AIDS.

The letter issued by the USCCB administrative board relates the "stories" of several PWAs. One is a woman with AIDS, another an intravenous drug user, another a gay man; and still another is a baby born with the disease. In response to these stories the bishops maintain that responses to AIDS need to be informed by adequate medical and scientific information (USCCB Administrative Board 1987, 483).

The Bishops define AIDS not as a "gay disease," but as a "human illness" affecting a wide variety of people. They make several recommendations concerning the civil rights and dignity of PWAs. The bishops call for compassionate treatment of the sick, oppose quarantining PWAs and mandatory AIDS testing, call on medical professionals to care for PWAs, especially in Catholic hospitals, pledge their support to collaborate with other social service and religious groups to care for PWAs, and call for further government funding for AIDS research and education and the expansion of programs and services for PWAs.

The bishops also call for an end to violence and discrimination against gays and lesbians, since all human beings deserve respect. Yet, unlike their concrete recommendations concerning AIDS legislation, they do not advocate any positive action to ensure justice toward gays (e.g., gay rights legislation). Also absent is the call for reconciliation with the gay community, which is present in the California bishops' letter. The bishops do not deal with issues of sexual morality when they discuss ministry to PWAs. Rather, they focus on care for the sick, since AIDS does not affect only gay men and may be transmitted through means other than sexual contact.

However, by separating the identity of PWAs as gay men from their identity as sick persons, the bishops uphold both a traditional ministry to the sick and a traditional condemnation of homosexuality. They feel free to call for allocation of government resources for AIDS research and patient care, and to speak out against discrimination against PWAs in housing, employment, and insurance. They endorse public education concerning AIDS transmission as a means of allaying fear of the disease as well as eliciting a more compassionate response toward the sick.

Although separating AIDS from homosexuality and defining it as a disease deserving of care and compassion serves to destigmatize PWAs, such a stance also allows the bishops to avoid discussing what their position on homosexuality might mean for gay PWAs. While the letter advocates pastoral ministry to PWAs, there are no guidelines as to what place church teaching on homosexuality has in this ministry. Such a position can be called "homophobic" in that it avoids dealing with the issue of gay lifestyle as it is embodied in sick persons, and separates church officials from the courtesy stigma of appearing to condone homosexuality. At the same time, the lack of explicit guidelines gives freedom of negotiation to priests at the local level when they are attempting to reconcile individual PWAs with the church.

In discussing AIDS prevention, the bishops mention intravenous drug use, but they focus on the sexual transmission of AIDS and uphold objective church teaching on sexuality. The bishops assert:

> Human sexuality is essentially related to permanent commitment in love and openness to new life. It is most fully realized when it is expressed in a manner that is as loving, faithful and committed as is divine love itself. That is why we call upon all people to live in accord with the authentic meaning of love and sexuality. Human sexuality, as we understand this gift from God, is to be genitally expressed only in a monogamous heterosexual relationship of lasting fidelity in marriage. (486)

The bishops further state that acting in accord with this understanding of sexuality is the only way to stop "a major source of the spread of AIDS." Thus, first they make no distinction between promiscuity and non-marital monogamy, especially as it exists in committed gay and lesbian relationships. All sexual acts outside of marriage, they contend, are immoral irrespective of their context. Second, all sex outside of marriage is portrayed as not only immoral but physically unhealthy, a view upheld by the Vatican and the California bishops.[5] Third, they claim that only heterosexual sexual relationships reflect divine love and are a proper expression of loving commitment. Finally, it can be inferred from the bishops' position that monogamous gay relationships are seen as inauthentic, less than truly human, and lacking in loving commitment. Despite the conciliatory stance the bishops have toward PWAs, there is no essential difference between the views on homosexuality expressed by the bishops and those issued by the Vatican.

The bishops make a pastoral concession in their firm stand, however, by allowing for the discussion of safer-sex practices in the context of AIDS education programs. Since their recommendations are directed toward American society as a whole and not simply to Catholics, the bishops believe their recommendations must reflect American pluralism. In allowing for the discussion of preventive measures such as prophylactics, the bishops maintain that they are simply providing factual information and not recommending the use of prophylactics.

The notion that the church would allow even the discussion of safer-sex guidelines was met with criticism from conservative laity and other American bishops, even though the letter clearly adheres to the church's position on sexual morality. One lay critic noted:

> If the bishops' paper on AIDS is accepted by all bishops, it represents a compromise with expedience, a triumph of practicality over traditional morality and a major shift in position. (Hale 1988, 171).

Hale notes that not all bishops accepted the letter's recommendation. One of the most vocal critics was Cardinal, then Archbishop, Mahony of the archdiocese of Los Angeles,[6] who noted that the bishops' statements on preventive education should not be understood as a "shift in the constant moral teaching of the Catholic church" (Archdiocese of Los Angeles, press release, 14 December 1987). In an effort to allay possible confusion over the letter, Mahony omitted the controversial passages before accepting it as a guide for the archdiocese's response to AIDS.

By holding a firm line on the church's objective teaching on sexual morality, American Catholic bishops, such as Mahony, maintain that the church cannot give the appearance of compromise. Rather, the image the bishops portray is of a constant, traditional, objective moral teaching on sexual issues imparted to the laity and the lower clergy from the pope and the bishops.

Compassion and Responsibility

In response to the controversy surrounding "The Many Faces of AIDS," the bishops of the United States adopted a new letter at their annual meeting. The document was titled *Called to Compassion and Responsibility: A Response to the HIV/AIDS Crisis* (National Conference of Catholic Bishops 1989). This document maintains the stance of compassion toward the sick that characterized the former document. It also reaffirms the traditional teaching on sexuality.

However, the document addresses areas not discussed in "The Many Faces of AIDS." The bishops speak to the issue of the church's teaching on homosexuality. They note that while gay men may be changing sexual practices, they are not living chaste lives in response to AIDS. Homosexual activity, the bishops maintain, is not a morally acceptable option. Yet they go on to condemn antigay violence.[7] The bishops also address the problem of HIV transmission among substance abusers, advocating drug treatment and HIV education targeted at intravenous drug users, but they do not advocate needle exchange programs as a public health measure. The bishops state that distribution of clean syringes would result in more drug taking and would send the "wrong message"—that substance abuse is socially and morally acceptable. The discussion of preventive education with regard to condom use was altered. Unlike the administrative board's document, *Called to Compassion and Responsibility* does not suggest that education programs discuss the use of condoms as a means of preventing the spread of HIV. Discussing condoms as an AIDS prevention strategy sends the wrong message also, the bishops assert, since such discussions do not dissuade people from nonmarital sexual relations. The bishops also state that discussing condom use is not a sound public health policy, because the failure rate of condoms is high. In this regard, the bishops once again use what appears to be a scientific legitimation for a recommendation reflecting their view of sexual morality.

The Hierarchy and Impression Management

As I have noted above, the Second Vatican Council attempted to make the church relevant and open to the modern world, rather than opposed to it. The council documents, particularly *Gaudium et Spes*, advocate an evolutionary or developmental approach to understanding reality, rather than a static worldview (Abbott 1966, 204); call for church teaching to respond to the "signs of the times" (Abbott 1966, 201); note the importance of scientific insights to the church's understanding of reality (Abbott 1966, 234, 246); and invite Catholics to collaborate with other religious denominations and all "men and women of goodwill" in alleviating social problems (Abbott 1966, 241, 355, 505) and promote a spirit of dialogue with "men [*sic*] of all shades of opinion" (Abbott 1966, 222, 245). However, this movement toward change, even more evident in the work of moral theologians following Vatican II, has not been reconciled with the traditional methodology and conclusions of official Catholic moral teaching (Cahill 1987, 196; Mieth 1987).

The pastoral letters on AIDS issued by both the California bishops and the bishops of the United States demonstrate the conflict between these two approaches. The bishops emphasize collaboration with all "people of goodwill" (USCCB 1987, 481) to help alleviate a social problem, note the importance of scientific knowledge in understanding the disease, and call for dialogue with those alienated from the church. The bishops' conciliatory stance and desire for just treatment of the sick and the alienated sets the tone for the letters.

Yet, when discussing the church's sexual morality, the hierarchy leaves little room for the values of openness and dialogue advanced by the council. The bishops shift from a pastoral and conciliatory stance to one of firmness in their role as official representatives of an uncompromising moral teaching. Charles Curran, in commenting on the firm position taken in official church teaching, notes:

> There is no doubt that a manualistic neo-scholasticism still reigns supreme in official Roman documents, especially in the area of sexuality. In the judgment of the majority of Catholic moral theologians writing today, this methodology is centered too much on the sexual faculty and the sexual act and fails to give enough importance to the total person and the personal relationships within which one exists. (Curran 1987, 275)

While Curran's analysis accurately reflects the methodology and conclusions of the Vatican letter on homosexuality, a rigid, act-centered theology also characterizes the firm stance on official moral teaching seen in the bishops' letters on AIDS. The bishops maintain traditional teaching and their authority as expert teachers in the church, but deploy attention from their firm position by clothing it in a rhetoric of conciliation (see Vaillancourt 1980, 286).

Bishops may hold views at variance with the official teaching, but they are not free to state these publicly.

Sweeney's (1992) survey of American bishops, for example, showed dissent within the American hierarchy on such issues as married clergy and the recall of married priests to active ministry. While Sweeney's work may be criticized for being methodologically flawed, his findings point to a heterogeneity of opinion among bishops. Rome attempted to silence Sweeney by forcing him to resign from his religious order.

When faced with even mild public dissent within their own ranks, the bishops tend to side with Rome, at least publicly. The lack of support for Archbishop Raymond Hunthausen in Seattle in 1986 is a prime example. The archbishop was censured by Rome for allegedly holding views on political, sexual, and liturgical issues that dissented from the magisterium (see Kung and Swidler 1987; Lernoux 1989). The American bishops made little effort to support the archbishop when they met in 1986 to discuss the matter. Rather, they primarily affirmed their loyalty to the pope and to church teaching.

Thus, in public pronouncements, the American hierarchy has called for compassion for the sick and even reconciliation for alienated gay people. Yet the bishops never waiver in their stand on sexual morality. On the informal level, as I will discuss in chapter 5, priests are freer in negotiating objective teaching in pastoral practice in order to reconcile alienated PWAs with the church.

4

Priests and AIDS Education

When priests minister to individuals, negotiation and conciliation generally take priority over upholding the church's objective teaching. As with the hierarchy, however, proclaiming church teaching becomes more significant in public contexts. Priests deemphasize the issue of sexual morality when they discuss pastoral ministry to PWAs. Yet, as organizational officials, many priests are firm about the need to present official teaching on sexuality in church-sponsored AIDS education programs. In this regard their response is similar to that of the bishops. Priests also feel free to exercise professional autonomy in the private sphere of pastoral ministry; however, they are more cautious about advocating pastoral accommodations in public situations, even on the pastoral level. The hesitancy of priests to discuss pastoral concessions in public settings reveals the limits of their professional autonomy. Official reprimands might result for priests advocating a stance at variance with that of their bishop.

Like the hierarchy, priests wish to distance themselves from nonrational explanations of AIDS by "blasting" (see Richardson and Cialdini 1981) those who define the disease as a divine punishment. Priests cultivate an image of prestige by associating themselves with medical definitions of

AIDS—"basking" in the reflected prestige of the medical establishment. They define PWAs as sick persons in need of care. They advocate preventive education that reduces fear and communicates medical information. Thus, priests attempt to portray the church as compassionate, socially relevant, and willing to cooperate with other social institutions in the fight against AIDS. By grounding their argument in the tradition and history of the church (see Hart 1973), they also seek to convince Catholic laity that compassionate treatment of the sick is an important organizational goal, but one that does not weaken the church's stance on sexual issues.

Priests also mirror the hierarchy in their disagreement over church involvement in preventive AIDS education. Priests are caught in the tension between their desire to protect public health through pastoral concessions in church teaching, on the one hand, and the need to uphold the church's official teaching on sexuality, on the other. While priests have more freedom to make pastoral accommodations on the private level, they feel greater ambivalence over what pastoral recommendations can be made in the public setting of church-sponsored AIDS education programs. Priests are more inclined to uphold the teaching of the church when they are discussing AIDS education programs than they are when discussing their response to AIDS as it is embodied in individual PWAs. That is, the stance priests take when speaking about what the faithful "should" do is different from the stance they take when ministering to a PWA who already has the disease.

Many priests do not advocate church involvement in disseminating all the relevant medical information regarding AIDS transmission. They believe the church should discuss only the means of AIDS prevention that support the church's teaching. While they note the need for the church to be involved in preventive education in the interest of public health, they do not endorse the discussion of such preventive measures as condom use in AIDS education programs, since condom use and other safer-sex practices presuppose promiscuous sexual activity.

However, preventive AIDS education that does not include all the factual information on the disease is not effective as a health recommendation. Brandt (1987, 202), in his historical examination of social responses to venereal disease, notes that attempts at changing behavior through fear and moralizing have consistently failed as mechanisms of public health. Brandt states that dissemination of complete health information is much better at effecting such changes. Yet, like many priests, the hierarchy does not advocate such rational educational measures. Pastoral accommodation on the public level might weaken official church teaching and the hierarchy's power to establish it.

Thus, the rationale for providing selective AIDS information goes beyond the need for sound health recommendations. Religious organizations in pluralistic societies rely on persuasive tactics when attempting to enforce organizational norms on constituents (Etzioni 1961; Scherer 1980). By endorsing only heterosexual monogamy in marriage as the alleged medically sound means of preventing AIDS, these priests encourage obedience to church teaching motivated by the fear of contracting a terminal illness, rather than through a rational and moral choice. Providing selective medical information helps to enforce church views, in that the possibility of contracting a life-threatening disease awaits those who do not conform to church teaching.

Many priests believe the faithful need to be protected from anything that could lead them astray from objective moral norms. This notion is paternalistic in that the laity are viewed as children who must be "protected" from the facts (Farley 1987). This perspective is based on a model of moral decision making in which the laity are not respected as moral agents who are capable of making an informed choice. Rather, the hierarchy makes pronouncements and the faithful are expected simply to comply.

Even individual dissent among priests on the church's sexual teachings does not always result in a belief that the church should compromise its teachings in public arenas.

Priests believe that official teaching should be proclaimed in these settings. While many of these priests allow for a lesser-of-two-evils approach in pastoral counseling situations, such as allowing gay men to live in monogamous unions and still participate in the life of the church, they do not advocate the same approach in AIDS education by advocating the discussion of safer-sex information as a public health measure.

Nevertheless, organizational officials, even on a public level, can be flexible within limits (Pruitt and Smith 1981). In the AIDS education debate, many other priests take a perspective different from the one noted above. They advocate discussing all the medical information on AIDS, including the mention of condoms, as a pastoral measure. This position reflects the one taken by the bishops of the administrative board of the USCCB (1987). Such recommendations give the impression that the church is willing to make rational, pastoral concessions in its objective teachings, but priests and bishops who advocate this position do not necessarily endorse a view that contradicts the magisterium's view on sex. These priests and bishops permit the discussion of pastoral measures without compromising on the ideal that the official teaching sets forth as normative. Church teaching itself and the ecclesiastical structure that promulgates it are not questioned. Yet the public discussion of pastoral concessions remains a point of conflict among church officials. The data from interviews with Los Angeles priests reveals the organizational conflict between firmness and accommodation in the public and private spheres.

A COMPASSIONATE RESPONSE

Priests whom I interviewed stated that teaching about the compassion of Christ was one of the best ways the church could refute attacks against PWAs. One priest maintained:

> An awful lot has to be done in our parishes because that's
> where the rank and file lives. A lot has to be done in edu-
> cation on the parish level. . . . It's very clear that we have
> to speak from the point of view of the gospel. What does
> Jesus say about the poor, those who are sick? Are we sup-
> posed to judge them, or isolate them, or neglect them, or
> be indifferent to them? Also we need to educate [Catholic
> people] to deal with their fears [about AIDS].

Several priests argued that care for the sick and outcasts
was at the heart of the church's tradition. They held that
PWAs are the modern-day "lepers" and that Christians need
to be compassionate toward them as Christ would be. Others
noted the example of St. Francis of Assisi, who is said to have
embraced a leper who represented Christ in disguise. AIDS
ministry, priests believed, should be framed as part of the
church's mandate to minister to the sick. Defining PWAs as
sick persons, while downplaying their identity as gay men,
would elicit a more compassionate response from Catholic
people. Many priests held that such education about Christian compassion in the face of the AIDS crisis should occur at
the grassroots parish level.

Priests noted the need for education to combat religious
and political extremists with regard to AIDS. One hospital
chaplain strongly asserted:

> In the issue of AIDS it is scandalous because so many
> Catholics are mouthing the stuff that's coming out of the
> evangelical corner of Christianity, which is totally incor-
> rect and unchristian insensitivity. So when Catholics are
> mouthing this stuff it's terrible.

This priest "blasted" Christian fundamentalists, such as Rev.
Jerry Falwell, who maintain that AIDS is the wrath of God on
homosexuals. Catholic people should reject such opinions,
he asserted. While none of the priests interviewed held that
AIDS represented a divine punishment, many noted the need

to refute this view. Another priest mentioned the need to combat the efforts of Lyndon LaRouche and his campaign to quarantine PWAs.

In contrast, priests "basked" in the Catholic response to AIDS, which they saw as much more compassionate and rational. They understood informational education as a way to combat the stigma caused by irrational fear of AIDS. One priest believed there needed to be a place in parish AIDS education for venting fears. At the same time, fear could be replaced with correct information on how the disease is transmitted.

Other priests mentioned the need to educate parish communities in ministering to PWAs. One priest noted that Catholic people on the parish level needed to know

> how to deal with people they might come in contact with who have AIDS and to help those people who do not have AIDS to help those who have the disease—pastoral ministry to AIDS people. One of the aspects that is very difficult to find in [educational] materials prepared by the public sector is the ministerial part. Everything is explicit and detailed on how you can get the disease but not much on how we can help them. I think that is the lack.

Another priest noted that efforts at AIDS education needed to include PWAs themselves "speaking and sharing their experiences and being part of the give and take." In this way, the AIDS crisis would become personalized and would not simply be an abstract entity. One parish priest noted that people could understand AIDS only if they identified with the stories of PWAs. He believed that many Catholics do not see AIDS as a problem that concerns them. Catholic people needed to consider what they would do if confronted with PWAs. In response, they should ask themselves: "Am I really a follower of Christ in these situations?"

Thus, priests, like the hierarchy, strongly advocated educating Catholic people about the organizational goal of ministering to the sick. They also advocated dissemination of medical information on AIDS to reduce irrational fears. However, in this context, such educational recommendations did not include discussing safer-sex guidelines. Rather they believed church-sponsored AIDS education should emphasize that AIDS is not contracted through casual contact. This information, they hoped, would lessen the stigma attached to AIDS.

PREVENTIVE EDUCATION

While bishops addressed the transmission of AIDS through intravenous drug use, albeit in a limited way, few priests even mentioned this issue. When addressing AIDS prevention, priests brought up the topic of safer sex, but differed as to the degree to which the church should be involved in such educational endeavors. Less than half the priests believed that the church should avoid discussions of safer sex or condom use. The church, they said, should advocate monogamy or abstinence. Priests gave a variety of reasons for holding this position.

A few priests noted that discussing medical information on AIDS prevention was inappropriate for the church. One priest stated:

> I don't think it's the church's place to teach safe sex. It is not our expertise to teach what works and doesn't work in handling this virus. I just don't think it's realistic to ask the church to back that. Common sense would dictate what you should do. The church should only be involved in preventive education when it acts for abstinence. There are too many groups already who can give information. We need to enter into the moral arena, not the medical arena. I don't think that's skirting the issue. We are not the only agency around that can teach about the medical issues. We witness to the gospel more clearly in the moral arena.

The church's expertise is in teaching morality, he maintained; yet the church should collaborate with AIDS service organizations, which are better equipped to teach about AIDS prevention. This priest avoided potential conflict between church teaching and pastoral recommendations through this division of labor.

Another priest stated that the church cannot discuss condoms or safer sex because of the confusion it causes. He stated:

> This recent letter from the American bishops, which has caused so much consternation and everything that the archbishop here has issued a whole clarification on it and has altered the text, is a sign of the problems that happen when you even hint that there might be an alternative approach.

This priest took the same position assumed by Mahony in halting educational programs targeted at the Latino community—that people will misunderstand if any means of prevention other than abstinence and monogamy are discussed (see chapter 3). To associate the church with a position of compromise raises questions concerning the immutability of official moral teachings. Such associations also make public accommodations in hierarchical teaching due to pastoral circumstances.

On a similar note, a priest in his early thirties held:

> There is only one brand of sexuality the church believes in, and that is between two people who are faithful to one another. I think the church should be consistent on it. The church is correct in its teaching that it is only abstinence or fidelity, and I think that anything else muddies rather than clarifies. I think the church should simply continue to be clear.

Discussing anything in an AIDS seminar or other church function that wavers from objective moral teaching would dilute the church's position in the eyes of the faithful. For these priests, the proper sphere for church involvement in AIDS education is in promoting its moral teaching. Disseminating information on the disease is proper for medical authorities. They believed that the church should present a consistent message in public educational settings. Like bishops, these priests believed that the church needs to remain firm in its "constant" official teaching on sexual issues. They upheld a clear boundary between making pastoral recommendations on an individual basis and making pastoral recommendations in public educational settings.

Other priests posited medical reasons for not endorsing the dissemination of information on safe sex or condom use. One priest who reported ministering to several PWAs stated:

> I don't know what is safe sex. How safe are condoms? Everybody seems to act as if condoms were the answer to the problem. No. Condoms don't really offer that much protection. . . . Anyone who watches the news and listens to all the findings finally becomes skeptical about the good news that they are hearing—safe sex? . . . And the Catholic church is an obstructionist institution because it won't go along with this; well then I really don't know what is the educational program in regard to safe sex that responsible people should get behind. I think there's a bandwagon approach to this presently.

He went on to say that engaging in "safe sex" was similar to playing Russian Roulette. He noted that it was a very dangerous game to play. For these priests, medical information on AIDS needed to be presented in church-sponsored AIDS education programs. However, safer sex was not a sure way to prevent AIDS and should not be discussed in church settings. This position eliminated the potential for conflict between church teaching and dissemination of medical information through presenting a medical fact—that safer-sex is not absolutely safe.

At the same time, a slight majority of priests differed from Mahony and backed the discussion of condom use and safer sex in church-sponsored forums. The objective norm was either abstinence or monogamy, but many Catholics did not live up to the ideal. Thus, the church had to advocate a lesser-of-two-evils approach to help avoid the spread of disease, even though this varied with the objective norms of church teaching. One priest in his thirties stated:

> I'm not so stupid as to believe people are going to believe what I say. We are weak people who make mistakes. . . . I want people to know that if and when they do, there's a safe way of doing it for all people concerned, not just to protect themselves, but to protect others.

He believed that the church should teach morality, but that there should also be a pastoral allowance for those who do not follow the church's teaching.

Another priest, who strongly upheld the church's objective teaching on sexuality, believed that the church's educational efforts would not reach simply Catholics. He held that people need to know all the means of prevention. Non-Catholics who did not follow the church's teachings in sexual morality should know all the means of prevention for their own protection and the protection of others. He made a distinction between the church's role as moral teacher and its role as public educator. However, church involvement in public AIDS education, he noted, should also include church teaching.

Other priests held that AIDS education was a matter of urgency; the church should get behind any strategies of education that are available. As one priest who ministered in a largely African-American parish mentioned:

> We can't even talk about condoms, and it's a matter of life and death. That's what should be going on, absolutely. We'd save people's lives, especially in the black and

> Latino communities. Especially in the Latino community, where the church is such a powerful influence. And we have to carry on this charade.

In the case of AIDS, the value of saving lives was greater than the church's objective teaching on sexuality, he believed. These priests advocated discussing safer-sex practices to avoid the greater evil of spreading a deadly disease. Although they did not advocate any sexual expression outside of marital monogamy, they called for a pastoral compromise.

A few priests believed that reticence to discuss condoms and safer-sex practices reflected the church's overall failure to deal with sexual issues. As one hospital chaplain mentioned:

> Really what is needed today on a broader scale is a theology of sexuality, not only the question of AIDS. What we are teaching and holding on to simply is not what people are accepting. In light of developments psychologically, sociologically, theologically, and spiritually, we have to update the church's teaching on sexuality. In fact, people are simply being turned off.

If the church failed both to reevaluate its theology and become more comfortable with the discussion of sexuality in general, Catholic sexual teaching would become more irrelevant to the lives of Catholic people. This priest, however, like other priests who dissented from official teaching on sexuality, still discussed the issue of safer sex as a lesser of two evils. The broader question of the inadequacy of church sexual teaching, while important, was not immediately relevant in the AIDS context. The practical and proximate goal of preventive AIDS education would be better served if they did not challenge official teaching, but rather were able to argue for preventive education by appealing to traditional theological categories.

EDUCATIONAL PROGRAMS

Priests cited the need for educational programs in Catholic schools and in adult education on the parish level. Several priests noted the need for AIDS education in minority communities. They believed that the church could play an especially effective role in AIDS education among Latinos. A priest who had worked in Latino parishes in Los Angeles stated:

> I think we have a certain amount of credibility in the Hispanic community that they do not give to other organizations. The Catholic church is one of the very few things they bring with them from Mexico that they find here. It's something familiar to them. So I think we do have a special entree there and of course a responsibility to educate them.

In this context, a few priests brought up the educational program canceled by the archdiocese of Los Angeles. One priest was critical of the lack of leadership in AIDS education shown by the archdiocese:

> There is not one church in the diocese that has done anything as a public forum, particularly in the black community. I don't know how I'd approach the whole matter. I have tried to find the information.

He bemoaned the fact that he could find no good educational resources sponsored by the church. He also stated that he hoped to hold an AIDS education seminar in his parish. Other priests noted that the archdiocese had taken a positive step in instituting AIDS awareness programs for priests.

While priests felt a need for parish-based AIDS education, none had provided such education in parishes. A few priests noted that they did not believe their parishioners would welcome the church's discussing AIDS education. As a pastor of a Latino parish stated:

> I suspect on a practical level that our congregation here, and we are not untypical, would not be pleased in the least to find a listing of safe-sex practices on a Sunday bulletin. So I think that is an idea before it's time, unfortunately.

These priests felt that lack of acceptance by the congregation kept them from implementing AIDS education on the parish level.

One priest noted that he had left AIDS information pamphlets in the church vestibule. Others stated that they prayed for PWAs at mass, or mentioned them in the context of a homily as an example of those to whom Christians should show compassion, but had not discussed AIDS in any other forum. Several priests did not believe their parish was greatly affected by AIDS and chose to devote their energies to other issues. One priest noted that if he were in a parish with a large gay population, then he would focus more attention on AIDS education. For this priest, as for many others, framing AIDS as an issue that largely affected gays made it a low priority for them since their parish did not have a large gay population.

Yet priests advocate educating the wider Catholic population to respond toward PWAs with compassion and to diminish irrational fears of the disease. They do not define AIDS as simply a gay issue when they discuss it. They also believe that the church should be involved in preventive education, but priests did not take the initiative in sponsoring educational programs on the parish level. Thus, priests had no experience in providing AIDS education, although they advanced several ideas as to what form educational programs should take.

AIDS PREVENTION AND THE CHURCH: A BRIEF NORMATIVE NOTE

Catholic church officials have advocated education for compassion toward PWAs and against irrational fear of AIDS. They have debated the issue of preventive education as well. Yet when data for this study were collected from priests in Los Angeles, the archdiocese had done little to implement AIDS education programs. Since that time more has been done in this area, but education about HIV prevention remains a thorny issue.

In debating AIDS education, American clergy in general have largely overlooked the issue of AIDS prevention among intravenous drug users and have focused their attention on sexual transmission of the disease. Moreover, while focusing on sexual transmission, church officials all too often have depicted the disease as affecting primarily gays and have not had the foresight to implement educational programs that could help prevent the spread of AIDS through heterosexual contact, especially in minority communities.

Delays in presenting effective AIDS education programs at the parish, diocesan, state, or even national levels are no doubt due, at least in part, to the continued debate over pastoral accommodations in public forums. For many priests and bishops, the practical agenda of providing AIDS education has priority over either upholding objective church teaching or reformulating the church's views on sexuality. Nevertheless, others believe that upholding a hard line on church teaching is essential. They do not accept the lesser-of-two-evils argument, even though this approach has a long tradition in Catholic theology.

For example, Curran (1982) notes that Catholic moral theology has traditionally made use of the lesser-of-two-evils model when norms are in conflict due to human sinfulness. The presence of sin in the world has justified actions that would not be acceptable if sin were not present. Curran cites the example of the just-war tradition. In the event that one nation threatens another and all peaceful means have been exhausted, then it is a nation's right to wage war in self-defense. Protecting the higher good is thought to outweigh the lesser moral wrong. This solution mediates between an objective moral belief in the sanctity of human life and the exigencies of the real world. Neither priests nor bishops would argue that the just-war tradition might lead the faithful to believe that killing is morally permissible. Yet many priests and bishops, when faced with the crisis of AIDS, do not accept the need for even the mention of safer-sex practices in preventive AIDS education programs. They believe Catholics and the broader society will think there has been a change in the church's "constant" moral teaching on sexual issues.

A refusal to accept pastoral accommodation on the AIDS education issue is not due to the church's failure to accept anything less than perfection from its faithful. As noted in chapter 1, sects may shut themselves off from the world and insist on in-group purity, but Roman Catholicism is a church (Troeltsch 1981) and as such has historically made accommodations when faced with social problems in its host society. Thus, insistence on maintaining a firm stance on the objective teaching of the church is rooted in both the historical moment and the nature of the issues under debate.

A great deal of controversy has surrounded official church teaching on sexual issues, particularly within American Catholicism.[1] Both the Vatican and many bishops in the United States have held a hard line on church teaching in the face of a constituency that increasingly questions church stands on such issues as artificial birth control, divorce and remarriage, abortion, and homosexuality. This crisis of authority is at the heart of the AIDS education debate. Many American Catholic churchmen, both bishops and priests, resist endorsing pastoral accommodations in public AIDS education forums because they want to appear uncompromising in their stand on sexual issues. Appearing to vacillate might compromise the firm positional commitment they have taken (see Pruitt and Smith 1981). At the same time, an insistence on firmness in the church's "constant" teaching represents an effort to protect the structure through which moral teaching is advanced. To appear to accommodate to a social issue and to the demands of the laity, particularly in the controverted area of sexuality, would weaken the position of bishops and priests as guardians of an immutable tradition defined by the hierarchy for the laity. The fact that many bishops and priests take an uncompromising stand on church sexual teaching in response to an often dissatisfied laity reveals the hierarchical desire to maintain control of Catholic moral teaching despite the dissent of the faithful on these issues.

5

Priests and PWAs

Proclaiming the "constant" teaching of the magisterium and ministering to those in need represent two organizational goals of the institutional church. As the official public voice of the church, the hierarchy firmly upholds its teaching on sexual morality. Priests, as the church's representatives in the informal context of pastoral ministry, make concessions in the objective teaching to achieve conciliation between the church and individuals.[1] Goffman (1959, 150) notes that mediators in an organization "guide the show" for the "managerial audience," yet translate management's views into a "verbal line" acceptable to the rank and file. Priests are those middlemen in the church structure who mediate between hierarchical directives and the concrete needs and life situations of the laity. Both the hierarchy and the laity become role partners with whom priests interact and who, at least in part, help determine the roles priests perform in their ministry.

Priests' status as both representatives of the church and as religious professionals authorizes them to carry out ministerial roles. As representative of the church, the priest is the "sacramental person" (Holmes 1971; Carroll 1981), the one who mediates the sacred. The priest has the authority to offi cially reconcile the individual with the church. This authority, however, is resident not in the individual per se, but in his office.[2] At the same time, priests see themselves as having an expertise as religious professionals, particularly as counselors, distinct from their roles as pastors or confessors.

Traditionally, pastoral counseling involved the "cure of souls," in which clergy directed the faithful to follow authoritative religious precepts (McNeill 1951). The goal of this spiritual direction was eternal happiness in heaven. While pastoral counseling continues to have a spiritual component, it has taken on a therapeutic dimension, in which the pastor has become a counselor of personalities.[3] The goal of counseling has become help and peace of mind in the here and now, rather than, or in addition to, salvation in the hereafter (Long 1981). By casting their counseling role in therapeutic terms, priests seek not only to help those they counsel, but to increase their own status as professionals. At the same time, the movement to therapeutic counseling is part of a shift from reliance on the authority of external principles as a guide for spiritual direction, to the authority of the internal experience of the individual.

Benson and Dorsett (1971) note the "structural conflict" between professionalization and bureaucratization in religious organizations. They discuss the opposition of collegial control to hierarchical authority, expertise to explicit rules, and flexibility to rigidity in the profession and bureaucracy, respectively. O'Neill (1968) examines this conflict specifically in terms of priests. The modern priest, he notes, is both a "promoter of freedom" for the people to whom he ministers, as well as "an agent of authority." As I noted in chapter 1, priests are lower-level officials in a hierarchical organization. They are licensed and mandated by the organization to carry out its work (see Hughes 1971). This structural constraint limits priests' actions in ministry but does not totally constrain them. Priests increasingly see themselves as religious professionals who, by virtue of their expertise, can act with autonomy in their ministry with lay "clients" while still defining their work as conforming to the organizational "charter" (Dingwall and Strong 1985).

While priests' status as professionals and as officials in a hierarchical organization presents the potential for conflict, such a potential also exists between priests' ministerial roles. Priests feel an obligation to both the official church and the persons to whom they minister. Thus they must negotiate between conflicting role expectations placed on them by both hierarchy and laity. Dewey (1971) notes that priests most often conform to the role expectations of their bishop, since the church is perhaps their most significant reference group. Yet, in the AIDS crisis, the hierarchy present priests with a "dual mandate" (see Coser 1979) both to uphold the church's teaching and minister to the sick. At the same time, priests desire to minister to PWAs who seek reconciliation with the church, even though they often dissent from the official teaching on sexuality.

Priests resolve these potential conflicts in a variety of ways. Sarbin and Allen (1968) note that through "instrumental acts" an actor tries to modify the conditions that cause role conflict—for example, segregating roles in time and space. Gay Catholic priests in Wolf's (1987) study segregated their roles as priests from their roles as gay men. In gay spaces (e.g., gay bars) they would act as gay men, but in religious spaces or in ministry situations they would act as priests. Priests in AIDS ministry distinguish between pastoral ministry to individuals and their role as public teachers. In the former, priests are free to be conciliatory and negotiate with the individual. In the latter, they are more constrained to hold the official views of the magisterium.

Another strategy discussed by Sarbin and Allen is "changing beliefs," which involves not so much a total change as a reorganization of beliefs so that conflict between roles is no longer seen. Actors may assign a priority to roles, as in Getzel and Guba's (1954) study of military officer-teachers who perceived themselves as either primarily officers or primarily teachers. In ministering to PWAs, priests exercise their teaching role when they inform PWAs of the church's teaching on the priority of conscience in moral decisions. In this way priests select which teachings they believe are appropriate in the ministerial situation. They also emphasize the status of the PWA as a sick person and give priority to their conciliatory roles (such as pastor or counselor) over their role as teacher.

Priests' recourse to the inner-directedness of their professional status also helps to mediate potential role conflicts. In seeing themselves as professionals, priests believe they have the autonomy to negotiate with individuals in pastoral cases. As Merton (1957) notes, not all potentially conflicting role partners are present at the same time. This "insulating mechanism" (Parsons 1952, 308) prevents potentially conflicting role partners from direct confrontation. Priests have freedom to act in the private setting of the "internal forum" without being observed by the hierarchy, a situation allowing priests' views about the autonomy of pastoral decisions to go unchallenged by hierarchical authority. The hierarchy and dissenting gay PWAs are also insulated from each other. Of course priests act within the confines of their understanding of the organizational charter. They also have the "unseen audience" (Goffman 1959) of the hierarchy symbolically present in interactions on the pastoral level, in that the priest knows his ministry is franchised by the bishop. Nevertheless, the absence of immediate hierarchical authority in pastoral settings sustains priests' impressions of professional autonomy, in spite of their position as lower clergy in the hierarchical structure. While inner-directedness gives priests a sense of control over religious production, their willingness to defer to the conscience of the individual allows PWAs to have a sense of control over their spiritual destinies as well.

Thoits (1987) holds that role conflict is resolved through negotiation between the self and others who may place conflicting role expectations on the actor. Role conflict may remain high in situations where flexibility in bargaining is low; conflict may be more easily resolved where bargaining flexibility is high. Similarly, Callero (1986) holds that conflict does not impede role relationships if there is enough agreement between role partners to "get the job done." Priests in AIDS ministry have enough flexibility in bargaining to have successful encounters with PWAs and still remain faithful to the organizational charter, thus attempting to satisfy both PWAs and the hierarchy.

Flexibility in negotiation is heightened when the negotiators believe they have limited time in which to achieve a compromise (Magenau and Pruitt 1979). In these cases they will accept more concessions than they would under circumstances with fewer time constraints. Yet negotiators risk losing an impression of firmness on official positions. Time constraints certainly exist in AIDS ministry, given the threat of death and loss of mental capacity posed by the disease. Because priests wish to help PWAs achieve reconciliation— for their own job satisfaction as well as for the benefit of PWAs—they often are more flexible concerning the church's teaching than they might be under other circumstances.

Furthermore, Etzioni (1961) notes that "individual deviance" is tolerated in normative organizations more often than "group deviance." The presence of an audience, or the "deviant's" links to groups not present in interaction, are relevant to the level of tolerance organizational officials will demonstrate. PWAs are terminally ill. In most cases they will not have the opportunity to publicize their negotiated reconciliation with the church. This situation may also allow priests greater freedom in ministering to PWAs.

MINISTERING TO THE NEEDS OF PWAS

Several roles comprise priests' role-set (Merton 1957). Fichter (1954) states that parish priests traditionally have held the roles of "mediator" (administering the sacraments and authoritatively speaking for God and the church) and "father" (giving personal and spiritual counsel). Writing in the 1950s, Fichter maintained that most large urban parishes in the

United States had lost the simplicity and personalism of these roles. Rather, priests had taken on many additional roles in the parish. Among these were administrator, businessman, civic leader, educator, and recreational director. Following the Second Vatican Council, however, lay religious professionals, volunteers, parish councils, and other parish committees have often assumed many of the priestly roles discussed above (Fischer 1987). Yet, Vatican II affirmed several roles for the priest, such as sacramental functionary, educator in the church's teaching, builder of Christian community, and pastor to the laity (see Abbott 1966, 535, 538–46). It is important to note that these official roles are based more on the status of the priest as representative of the church or servant of the people of God than on the priest's status as a professional.

The roles priests play depend not only on the context (e.g., public rituals, social action, or individual ministry) but also on the needs of the others with whom priests interact. Role-taking (Mead 1934), that is, adopting the standpoint of the other, shapes the roles actors use in relating to another (Turner 1956). Actors' beliefs about the status characteristics (Berger, Rosenholtz, and Zelditch 1980) of another also circumscribe role selection. When discussing AIDS ministry, priests mention roles they believe will meet PWAs' needs. Conversely, priests enumerate only those needs they believe they can fulfill. In other words, priests discuss the spiritual and psychosocial needs of PWAs but rarely mention PWAs' financial or physical needs. The dual status characteristics of PWAs as both sick and gay also influence the roles priests anticipate using when interacting with PWAs. Thus, before discussing how priests define their ministerial roles, it is necessary to note how they define or organize the status of PWAs and how they perceive PWAs' needs.

Taking the Role of PWAs

Only five priests stated that PWAs had no unique needs. The ministerial needs of PWAs, they maintained, would be identical to those of any other person dying of a terminal illness. As one priest who had not ministered to PWAs stated:

> We are treating them as something different, and that creates a barrier in itself. I think they should be treated like any other person who has a terminal disease. . . . A person with leukemia or cancer has to go through the dying process. They have to be helped through that process. I think the PWA also has to be helped through that process.

This priest believed that ascribing special needs to PWAs served only to segregate them from the rest of society and to heighten the stigma of AIDS. Ascribing special needs to PWAs would hinder ministry to them. At the same time, as I have noted with regard to the hierarchy's response to AIDS, defining PWAs only as sick persons allows clergy to ignore the difficult questions concerning church teaching on homosexuality.

In contrast, the majority of priests believed that PWAs had unique needs, particularly since the majority of PWAs were gay men. These priests noted that, in their experience, PWAs were terminally ill young men, stigmatized by society and often alienated from the church and their families. These factors set PWAs apart from persons suffering from other terminal illnesses.

Nine priests mentioned that the youth of PWAs was one factor that set them apart from most other terminally ill people. One priest in his sixties noted:

> It must be terrible to know that you are young, as many of these people are. As one of them said to me, "I always knew I was going to die, but I didn't know I would die so young. There are many things I want to do, and I just won't get a chance to do them."

This priest noted that the majority of PWAs have not been able to achieve their life goals, nor have they had the comfort of looking back over full and long lives. Such a situation, priests maintain, often makes it difficult for a PWA to accept death. Since PWAs often die young, one priest noted:

> There's a lot of recrimination against God for this vengeful thing which is happening in their lives. . . . There is a lot more pain and sorrow involved with these than a lot of other deaths. A lot of it has to do with the fact that the person dying is usually pretty young. He hasn't lived a full life yet.

In this priest's experience, PWAs may blame God for their disease and feel anger and hostility about dying young.

The majority of priests mentioned that PWAs had to deal with alienation or social stigma to a much greater degree than other terminally ill people. Over one-third of the priests noted the stigma attached to AIDS. Over one-third also mentioned feelings of alienation from the church as being unique to gay PWAs, while seven priests felt that PWAs were often alienated from family, friends, or lovers. Priests discussed the sexual orientation of PWAs as a reason for greater conciliation between PWAs and the church. Yet few discussed the church's official condemnation of homosexual acts. Priests focused on individual reconciliation on the informal level.

A priest who worked in a largely Hispanic parish noted the social stigma attached to AIDS:

> People afflicted with AIDS are coming out of a lifestyle of either homosexuality or drug use, something that has marginalized them, has put them at odds with "proper society." There's a lot more to deal with by way of isolation, alienation, loneliness, the frustration of not having a recognized support system—sort of a whole atmosphere of illegitimacy and moral judgment seems to be weighing on many of these people. I don't think that would be the case with the average person suffering

from cancer or something like that. In a sense it's socially okay to have them, and you get 100 percent compassion from society. With AIDS I don't think we're anywhere near there as far as a compassionate society is concerned.

From this priest's perspective, the added stigma of homosexuality or drug abuse compounded the stigma of disease and isolated PWAs from the rest of society.

Many priests claimed that the majority of gay PWAs were alienated from the church because of their sexual orientation and needed reconciliation. One young parish priest who had experience ministering to PWAs in a hospital setting stated:

Frequently there is a tenuous connection with the church. The homosexuality question apart from AIDS creates a whole different spirituality. So often the homosexual feels rejected, and some of them will react with guilt and some of them will react with incredible anger. Some will react with both.

This priest noted that while PWAs often feel isolated from the church, most Catholics with terminal illnesses do not feel this isolation. On a similar note, another priest stated:

Remember, a lot of people dying from AIDS, especially in the gay community, are very bitter and broken and have a lot of feelings toward the church that are not real positive. So a lot of times the first person they ask for will not be a priest, and sometimes they will; it depends on where the person is standing with the church at the time that they are sick.

This priest maintained that PWAs often rejected ministry by a priest and that the church needed to build bridges to alienated PWAs. Another priest noted that gay practicing Catholics often served to initiate a reconciliation between the church and their disaffiliated gay Catholic friends who had AIDS.

Several priests also noted that PWAs were often alienated from families, friends, or lovers. A priest who had volunteered to work with an AIDS organization and had extensive experience in AIDS ministry stated:

> Quite a few of them [PWAs], their families have rejected them and don't want anything to do with them, and they have that whole thing to deal with, which a lot of times is more important to them than the disease they are dying with. Somehow, if that could be resolved, if they could get their family to somehow accept them before death arrives, then, at least with the people I have worked with, that's the more important. Most of the other times you don't get rejected by your family because you have cancer or something like that, but with this disease, because there is still a lot of social stigma that goes along with it, the family is not there to give them the support, and sometimes friends aren't around either.

When someone is stricken with a terminal illness, this priest believed, the family and friends are often drawn closer to the sick individual. But when a person becomes ill with AIDS, he is often abandoned by family and friends.

A parish priest noted a different situation in his experience:

> I dealt with two guys who were basically out on the street because their lovers found out they had AIDS. These were the situations where they went back to the family. They had no place else to go.

This priest ministered to these PWAs because their families were members of his parish. He maintained that the families had accepted these PWAs because they had already come to terms with their sexual orientation before they became ill. Often, priests noted, the family discovers the PWA's sexual orientation only when the PWA discloses his illness.

At the same time, several priests noted that they were impressed by the level of care family and friends gave to PWAs. In a few cases priests also discussed a lover's concern for the PWA. Generally, however, priests rarely mentioned dealing with a PWA's lover. Rather, they discussed their experiences with the PWA's biological family or his friends.

In the midst of the alienation and loneliness PWAs experience, priests claim, PWAs need reconciliation with their families and with the church to experience a peaceful resolution of their lives. A priest who had been involved in AIDS ministry for four years asserted:

> These men want very much to tell someone in the church their story—their loves, their passions, their wounds, their glorious moments, and moments of doubt, their beautiful moments.

For this priest, listening to a PWA's story was a step in bringing reconciliation with the church.

Another priest who had extensive experience in AIDS ministry summed up his perception of PWAs' needs in this way:

> With this disease, the love, support, and acceptance are so important because it's the new leprosy and the person feels that—that nobody wants to be in the room [with them]. Does anybody want to be near him; does anybody want to touch him? To make him feel lovable, touchable, I would say that's important. The presence, loving, touching, being close to them.

Priests mentioned PWAs' need to talk or to be touched by family, friends, or even a representative of the church in order to ease their feelings of abandonment.

Many priests stated that PWAs internalize social stigma and experience guilt because of their disease. One priest related a story of a gay man who told no one he had AIDS due to his shame over the illness:

> Part of what that did for me . . . was help me to really appreciate how ashamed some people can feel about having the disease. . . . And it's difficult enough to be sick and terminally ill—but to have it from something one also associates with some sort of badness.

The linkage between AIDS and a socially disvalued behavior caused PWAs to experience guilt.

Priests most often mentioned that certain PWAs felt that God was punishing them for their sins. While priests noted that other terminally ill people may feel they are being punished by God, these feelings are especially acute for PWAs. Another priest stated:

> AIDS is an experience of inevitable dying, but the thing that complicates it is: What's the meaning of this death? Is there some hidden meaning to it because our Western socicty has considered homosexuality a perversion that is punished by God? That's the image behind it.

The moral opprobrium accompanying homosexuality, this priest maintained, heightened the likelihood that PWAs would experience guilt because of their disease. A priest who reported ministering to several PWAs claimed:

> A significant number, not a majority, a number of them wonder if their illness is not a punishment from God; there must be an assurance that there is not a direct relationship between AIDS and God's judgment.

PWAs, he believed, needed assurance that AIDS was not God's punishment. No priest mentioned that he believed

AIDS represented a divine punishment, and priests often defined their views as distinct from fundamentalist Protestantism. Another priest who had also ministered to several PWAs remarked:

> In one of the stages with all of these guys, they want your assurance as a priest that they are okay. As any person who is dying is okay in the eyes of God.

This priest believed that if a PWA thought AIDS was a divine punishment, then he needed the opinion of a representative of the church to help dissuade him from that belief. This priest sought to assure PWAs that they were accepted by God and the church.

One priest noted:

> A lot of times people with AIDS feel, "My God, this is the end, and not only is it the end, but I'm going to go to hell too." They will have very much of that hell-fire-and damnation thing.

Several priests stated that PWAs needed assurance not only that their disease was not a sign of divine judgment, but that they were not going to hell. Rather, PWAs needed to maintain a sense of hopefulness in a seemingly hopeless situation.

Priests define PWAs as sick persons, oppressed by society and in need of care. Even when they note the sexual orientation of PWAs, they mention it as a source of alienation and not as a "sinful lifestyle." Priests bring up the issue of sexual morality only when they directly discuss the relationship of the church's teaching to their ministry with PWAs.

Priests project a conciliatory and accepting image of the church. They see themselves as agents of reconciliation between the church and alienated PWAs. They also see themselves as possessing the professional counseling skills needed to help PWAs accept their illness and to achieve reconciliation between PWAs and their families.

Roles in AIDS Ministry

Nearly half the priests understood their status as religious professionals and official representatives of the church as legitimating their ministry. A priest who reported extensive experience in AIDS ministry stated:

> A priest who comes from the outside comes with the credentials and the objectivity that nobody else around them seems to have. They [PWAs] appreciate that.

PWAs, he maintained, saw priests as religious professionals who could objectively assure PWAs they were accepted by God. Family members and friends did not possess that objectivity.

One young priest stated:

> Well, a priest represents the church in a very profound way for people. It's one thing to have lay eucharistic ministers coming to bring the sacrament, but the priest somehow symbolizes that person who is the church. Any reconciling or anything the church can do for that person would fall in the responsibility of the priest. Anybody can sit and listen to their problems and give advice and all that, but it's our responsibility to be the church to them.

Priests believed their role was unique in that they represented the authority of the church to PWAs. Laypeople could not represent the church in the same way. As representatives of the official Church, priests saw themselves as building bridges between PWAs and the church.

Priests combine their self-understanding as representatives of the church and as religious professionals in defining appropriate roles for AIDS ministry. Among these are the roles of companion, befriending PWAs; therapeutic counselor; spiritual guide; and sacramental minister. These roles are conciliatory or pastoral. That is, they are roles in which priests accept PWAs as sick people. Priests are also teachers, however, a role that carries a potential for conflict.

Companion.   A ministerial role discussed by one-quarter of the priests was simply to visit, talk with, and touch PWAs. This role helped fulfill the PWA's need for companionship in the face of social isolation. Priests reported that PWAs appreciated someone who was not afraid to hold their hand or embrace them. One priest who had friends with AIDS, but had not "officially" ministered to a PWA as a priest, stated:

> I think just the normal human stuff is what I would want to bring into ministry. They don't want magic words or solutions or theologizing.

A priest who had been involved in AIDS ministry for three years maintained that when he ministered to PWAs he would

> try to communicate to them my acceptance and love and show them there is no rejection. I would try to be there as a person who is just present to them.

Priests believed that this ministry of presence would help PWAs feel they were not rejected by the church. As representatives of the church, priests, through their ministry of friendship, would help PWAs trust the church and provide a first step in achieving reconciliation. One parish priest reported his experience with a PWA:

> Up to four or six weeks ago he didn't want to see a priest. I used to go and visit, but I would go in "civi" clothes and as a friend of his mother's. I always told him any time you want to talk to a priest don't hesitate to call. I tried to be a friend rather than a person with a collar who had been an offense to him when he was nineteen years old and left the church. He had been

away from the church for about twelve years, but in the last few weeks there has been some reconciling. He seems to be more comfortable with God; he has received the eucharist a couple of times, so I suspect there has been some healing.

This priest distinguished his role as friend and visitor from that of "official" minister. Relating to the PWA as a friend provided a bridge to further ministry and reconciliation with the church. There was no mention of the church's teaching on homosexuality in this context. Rather, this priest wished to change the PWA's negative image of the official Church.

Therapeutic Counselor.   Ten priests discussed their ministry to PWAs in terms of therapeutic counseling. Priests, they noted, act as facilitators who help PWAs work through problems, or accept death. Often, priests saw themselves as employing a nondirective approach. These priests did not impose authoritative answers on PWAs, but rather allowed PWAs to come to their own resolutions concerning emotional and spiritual issues. One priest who reported ministering to several PWAs stated:

> I want to be there to facilitate before their dying, to articulate the wonders and mystery of their own life.

This priest went on to state that his role was that of a listener. He would urge PWAs to tell their stories and help them "to go through the passage of death in a very peaceful, happy kind of way."

Similarly, another priest who had ministered to only a few PWAs recounted:

> Generally my pastoral response in any of these cases has been to help people to wrestle, to stay with it, and to experience a breakthrough, a conversion, moving through it to a place of centeredness a place of peace. And really

believing that people have the resources, the power within them. We all have the power within us.

This priest saw one of his ministerial roles as helping the PWA to accept his disease and resolve any bitterness he had toward his family or the church. In coming to this "place of peace," the PWA not only would have a more peaceful death, but would experience a more peaceful life in the time he had remaining.

Priests also saw their ministry as helping families of PWAs cope with the illness. One priest reported:

> The parents don't want to accept that [their son has AIDS] and deny it. . . . That's where you have the hardest job. You have to say: "Hey, you're doing more damage to yourself at this time than to the person who has AIDS, because you're denying and destroying yourself from within rather than accepting what has happened and making the best of the time that remains."

Priests believed that they could help families accept both a PWA's illness and the fact that their son was gay.

Spiritual Guide. Beyond a role as therapist, eighteen priests saw themselves as spiritual counselors helping PWAs achieve peace with God. Seven priests specifically mentioned their role of helping PWAs prepare for life after death. In this context, priests focused on PWAs' status not as gay men, but as sick persons. One parish priest defined his role as

> helping them to struggle with a bigger reality, ultimate questions—I think a priest is there to be center stage in that. With AIDS they are dealing with those bigger questions. You have to be compassionate to their misery.

A priest, he maintained, had a unique role in dealing with ultimate questions and trying to reassure the PWA of God's love. A parish priest who had ministered to several PWAs also stated:

> If they are open to talk to a priest or minister, then we should be there ready and willing to talk with them and not be afraid to talk with them, and to talk with them about death and the approach of death. It's not the fear of dying, but the love of God for them and how God is looking forward to welcoming them home into the kingdom of heaven. . . . So my role is to get them emotionally set and spiritually set for their ultimate death, so I have to play an important part in their spiritual and emotional [preparation].

The role of the priest, he believed, was to help the PWA face death with hope in eternal life.

Three priests mentioned that the suffering that PWAs endured brought them closer to God. As one of them stated:

> We have within our tradition a theology of suffering which never asks for suffering, but when it is experienced, to understand it not as punishment but as another avenue toward sanctification.

This priest saw the suffering of PWAs not as a divine punishment, but as the vehicle by which the PWA could achieve sanctification.

Sacramental Minister.　The role where the priest acts in his most official capacity as the representative of the church is in the administration of the sacraments. Even when discussing this role, however, priests focused on reconciliation between the church and the PWA, rather than the church's official teaching on homosexuality. The sacramental role was seen as significant to AIDS ministry by nearly half the priests. Generally, priests exercised their role as sacramental minister during hospital visitations. In two cases priests baptized PWAs. Other priests mentioned giving communion to PWAs and hearing their confessions. Priests most often mentioned celebrating the Sacrament of the Sick, a rite to bring the individual comfort during illness. Priests noted that the administration of the sacraments could help bring about spiritual and emotional healing. Even physical healing could be improved. One priest asserted:

> The Sacrament of Reconciliation is in itself, or can be, a part of the healing process of a person who is hurt. I think many priests do not take that into account. We have a long tradition of praying for physical, spiritual, and emotional sickness, but we don't take it into account. I myself do it. Why not?

Priests believed, however, that emotional and spiritual healing could occur not only through administering the sacraments but through their roles as therapeutic and spiritual counselors as well.

In fact, priests believed that simply administering sacraments was a minimal and insufficient ministry to PWAs. A hospital chaplain who reported having ministered to several PWAs noted:

> It isn't enough to simply come in and do the sacraments. I think that is really poor, minimal hospital ministry. I celebrate sacraments, but its not the primary ministry with any patient. I think reconciliation, education, trying to deal with people's fears are far more beneficial where time allows. Then spiritual ministry is much more effective.

This priest believed that his ministerial roles included more than administering sacraments.

Priests did not want to be seen simply as sacramental functionaries. They often mentioned that they were called to minister to the sick only when a PWA was near death. They expressed frustration that they were not called sooner so that they might be more effective in helping to counsel the PWA. A priest in his sixties who had ministered to several PWAs complained:

> With some people I think there's that hesitancy, that reluctance in general, particularly until that last moment of death. You know, when the priest comes that means the very end. We're still stuck with that mentality of sacramentality of the "last rites." So unfortunately, with AIDS or non-AIDS, many people, friends, and family members, the first contact is when it's literally the last moment.

Many PWAs, priests believed, understood the priest's role only as someone who would perform the sacraments of the church while they were dying. Priests believed they could have an important role as counselors in assisting the PWA through the dying process. They also saw themselves as important mediators between the PWA and family members. This lack of role recognition on the part of PWAs, their families, and friends caused priests frustration.

CONFLICT IN MINISTRY

All the roles noted above allow priests to act as agents of conciliation toward PWAs. Yet when priests counsel PWAs, they have occasion to proclaim the church's official views on sexual morality. A potential for conflict exists between priests' conciliatory roles and their role as teachers. In ministry to PWAs priests must negotiate between these roles in order to successfully minister to PWAs and successfully represent the church. Only three priests did not recognize the potential conflict between these roles. Yet even these priests used a strategy that blocked conflict.

Most priests felt a duty to defend or at least present the church's moral teaching on homosexuality to a gay PWA who would question it. One priest noted: "I have two roles that cross, the pastoral and the teaching." While he maintained that his ministry was "not licensed for private practice," and that he had a duty to present church teaching, he questioned how he could apply the church's views on homosexuality in ministerial situations.

Most respondents believed they had a duty to uphold the teaching of the church, but they also noted the dual mandate given them by the hierarchy to minister to PWAs. As a young priest maintained:

> I think it was unfair that people picketed the pope [in San Francisco], . . . but that did not dissuade him from proclaiming God's love to those with AIDS; he came and touched them. He is adamantly for church doctrine, but as far as the human person is concerned, you saw his compassion. As far as the person dying of AIDS, there's the compassion.

This priest saw his desire to minister to PWAs as a response to the pope's example. All respondents believed that in ministering to PWAs they would be answering the hierarchy's call for compassion.

Yet priests must also meet the expectations of the PWAs to whom they minister. One priest who worked with the gay community for several years expressed anger over the Vatican document on ministry to homosexual persons (Sacred Congregation for the Doctrine of the Faith 1986):

> As somebody who works with the gay community and PWAs and their families, that document angered me because it interfered with my work. It opened old wounds, and as a priest I get identified with some of that. And some of that wrath came my way, because there's no one else that person is going to talk to. I've

> seen parents hurt by that document. They would be at peace with their son, and then when the document came out they see this great authority speaking and . . . all their doubts are back. They say; "Are you just being radical and departing from the teaching?" How do they deal with this document, which says that their son is intrinsically oriented toward evil? That all his relationships, all he is doing, is directed toward evil?

This priest saw his identification with the church hierarchy as an impediment to his work with the gay community. He attempted to dissociate himself from church teaching and convince PWAs that they did not need to accept church teaching to be reconciled with the church. The majority of priests, however, did not wish to dissociate themselves from the hierarchy or church teaching. Regardless of their personal assent or dissent from the magisterium's positions, they had an obligation to present them.

One priest noted the need for presenting the church's teaching in a "positive" rather than condemning light:

> The positive statement the church is trying to make in the statements [on homosexuality] is that sexuality fully has its home in a faithful, committed, married, heterosexual relationship, open to the transmission of life. Sexuality fully has its home there. Anything other than that is in some way deficient. Not necessarily to use that term *deficient* in a pejorative, guilt-inducing, finger-pointing sense, but isn't really quite what it should be. But then again, most of us live our lives in every area as not really, by various objective standards, what they should be. Our lives in every aspect are lived somewhere under the ideal.

By presenting the official teaching in conciliatory terms, this priest presented an impression of the church as tolerant and accepting. Still, he would attempt to persuade PWAs that even monogamous gay sexual relationships were morally deficient.

In negotiating with PWAs on the pastoral level, priests discussed two strategies to avoid or reduce role conflict: (1) giving priority to one role or group of roles, or (2) compartmentalizing roles. These strategies facilitate priests' negotiations between role partners. They also soften the impression of church teaching that priests convey to PWAs. Even though the majority of priests stated they would at least discuss church teaching, they noted that ultimately they would defer to the conscience of PWAs and help reconcile them with the church.[4]

Role Priority

The majority of priests held that they resolved or would resolve role conflict by ministering in both their pastoral and their teaching roles, but would give one priority over the other. Only three priests saw their role as teacher as having priority. The others saw their pastoral roles as more important than their role as teachers. Priests differed, however, in the importance they gave their teaching role in ministerial situations.

Nine respondents held firm on the church's teaching but attempted to achieve a compromise. They stated that they had been, or would be, very directive in their counseling of PWAs and would attempt to convince them of the church's teaching as a moral ideal. One priest who did not have experience ministering to PWAs noted:

> I think in our society we always have to be calling people to something greater, not to let them be content with only getting half way there, getting part way there to some goal. That is my understanding of my preaching, my ministry as a priest.

However, since all Christians fall short of the ideal, this priest believed that PWAs involved in a gay lifestyle could be reconciled to the church. Yet he wanted them to accept the church's teaching as the ideal, even though they did not live up to it.

Seven respondents believed they had a duty to state the church's viewpoint on sexual morality but would not attempt to convince PWAs of the correctness of this teaching. PWAs had to decide for themselves what they believed. One of these priests stated:

> What I have to do for people is to express to them what the teaching is of the Catholic church. One of the essential elements is that the individual has to come to grips with acting out of his conscience. My duty is to give you the teaching. My duty is not to force you to accept my teaching, but to help you form your conscience. And as you live your life, you live it according to your conscience, which has been informed with the teaching of the church.

This priest believed that once he had articulated the church's position to the PWA, he had fulfilled his obligation as the representative of church teaching. His desire to minister to the PWA took priority over his teaching role. Also, the inner-directedness of the individual PWA had priority over objective church teaching.

Five priests noted that they felt no responsibility to uphold church teaching when ministering to PWAs. These priests attempted to make the church appear more acceptable to gay men who might feel alienated or rejected by traditional proscriptions against homosexuality. One priest who had worked extensively with PWAs stated:

> Catechesis is important to update people in what they learned at an earlier time in their lives and because they have become somewhat distanced from organized religion. When they are reconciled, it's good to bring them up to date on some areas. One of the main things

is to relieve them and inform them about a much more correct attitude about homosexuality. I think that's a basic issue. That's simply the stuff we've gotten, and a terrible misunderstanding and judgmental attitude shown to gay people are simply not based in good biblical scholarship.

This priest did not believe that the official teaching of the church was the ideal, and he believed that priests should teach PWAs that there are voices in the church that accept a gay lifestyle as moral. He advocated explaining the positions of moral theologians who disagreed with the official teaching, but downplayed discussing the teaching itself.

A minority of priests gave priority to their teaching role over their pastoral roles. These priests had no experience with AIDS ministry. One priest stated that he would be compassionate and understanding to a gay PWA who recognized that his lifestyle was sinful. He asserted:

> We are sinful by nature. We have to allow other people that possibility of sinning and help people understand the completely forgiving love of God.

Yet this priest maintained that a PWA who dissented from church teaching and was in a monogamous union with another man would have to repent of that relationship before he could be reconciled with the church.

Role Separation

Priests who gave priority to the teaching role also separated their role as pastor in ministering to PWAs from their teaching role. These priests saw PWAs as sick persons in need of ministry. They did not mention PWAs' status as gay men. Yet, when faced with the issue of a gay PWA dissenting from the church's teaching, they maintained a rigid view of their role as representative of the church's official teaching.

In all, twelve priests separated their pastoral role from their teaching role. These priests did not see the role of teacher as generally relevant in AIDS ministry. As a hospital chaplain stated:

> I don't see my role as educating someone about the teaching of the church when they are dying. I don't see any conflict at all. . . . In another context I have a responsibility to teach.

This idea was echoed by another priest, who stated that in a situation of pastoral ministry he did not have to explain the church's moral teaching: "I don't have to be in the pulpit," he maintained. These priests saw a difference between their pastoral role, exercised in private settings, and their teaching role, exercised in public settings such as preaching at mass. In the former, priests had the freedom to be more conciliatory; in the latter, they proclaimed the teaching of the magisterium.

Priests saw their role as helping a terminally ill individual come to the end of his life with the assurance of God's love. A priest who also had ministered to PWAs recounted an experience where a PWA asked, "Am I going to heaven?"

> He wanted to hear that. He wasn't hearing it from his father [a Baptist minister]. I said "Why not? Are you not a good person? . . . You are a good person. God knows that. He's not looking at labels of whether you're gay, straight, or anything else. You try to love people." In one of the stages with all of these guys they want your assurance as a priest that they are ok, as any person who is dying is ok in the eyes of God. If I can give them that when they are ready for that; I'm there for that. I seem to be the only one who can give them that. Their mothers are gonna tell them they're wonderful no matter, doctors avoid the question, friends will say yes to whatever they want them to say. A priest who comes

from the outside comes with the credentials and the objectivity that nobody else around them seems to have. They appreciate that.

This priest did not discuss the teaching of the church on homosexuality in the pastoral setting. Rather, he assured a dying person of eternal life and presented a conciliatory image of the church. This stance also helped him to have a successful and rewarding encounter with a PWA.

Another priest, when asked how he might integrate his teaching role with his pastoral roles, maintained:

> I don't think there is a problem or question at all in terms of ministering to PWAs, as there would be no problem in ministering to someone with cancer. Someone has a life-threatening illness and is in need of the ministry the church has to offer. Where that question becomes more relevant is when I'm ministering to someone who is dealing with their homosexuality, and trying to figure out how active they are going to be, and what I do is present what the church teaches and why. And the church has a whole body of teaching on conscience.

This separation of the teaching role from the pastoral role reveals a separation of the status of PWAs. These priests perceived them only as sick individuals and not as gay men. In this way, the issue of homosexuality was separated from AIDS ministry for these respondents.

Conscience

Apart from the strategies noted above, a large majority of priests also avoided conflict between roles by deferring to the conscience of the individual to whom they were ministering. Even priests who attempted to convince PWAs of the church's teaching would ultimately accept the PWA's decision to either embrace or reject the magisterium's views on homosexuality. Priests believed that by accepting a decision made in conscience they were being faithful to their roles as both pastors and teachers. As a priest who had been ordained twenty years stated:

> What I have encountered with a lot of people is that they hear the teaching of the church and they put that into perspective in their own life as they are dealing with a serious relationship with someone else, . . . if they come back to me and say, is that right or wrong? All I can say to them is, what does your conscience say to you? If your conscience tells you it's right even though I tell you it's wrong, you are responsible to live your life. It's kind of a weasel approach and kind of a legalistic approach, but it allows me as a pastoral minister to care for the people without being judge, jury, and executioner.

Deferring to the conscience of a PWA allowed this priest to act as a counselor while still upholding the organizational charter. Maintaining a hard line in ministerial situations would have impeded successful ministry with PWAs.

Other priests maintained that by instructing PWAs about the church's belief about the priority of conscience in moral decision making, they were in fact fulfilling their role as teachers. As one young priest asserted:

> The church has given me an out. It's only in a one-on-one kind of relationship that I am permitted to do that. I have to call the person to understand the church's teaching to the best of their ability, then I am obliged to tell them that the ultimate norm of morality is the well-formed conscience. They know what the church says and what the church teaches, and now they must follow their own conscience. Then the person says, "This is the best I can accomplish," or the person says, "I don't

believe this is wrong," then I have to allow that to happen, having educated them to the best of my ability about why the church says what it says. When a person arrives at their conclusion, having done everything possible they could, having studied everything they could, then I have to give them the room to do that. . . . The church's teaching says that the ultimate moral norm is your conscience well informed.

This priest noted the ambivalence of his conflicting roles. Priests made use of the church's teaching on conscience to help redefine their role as teachers of the church's sexual morality.

SUMMARY

Priests believe they have the resources and the expertise to meet the needs of PWAs. They act as companions, therapeutic counselors, spiritual guides, and sacramental ministers. In all these roles, priests seek to help PWAs come to terms with their illness and achieve reconciliation with the church. Yet the organizational goals of ministering to those in need and upholding church teaching conflict when priests minister to gay PWAs. However, priests were able to overcome this structural ambivalence.

While priests generally believe they have an obligation to proclaim church teaching, they feel free to reconcile PWAs with the church even if PWAs do not assent to official teaching on homosexuality. Priests' relative professional autonomy is reflected in their willingness to negotiate with PWAs in ministerial situations. Yet, as I note in chapter 1, negotiating with alienated constituents also falls to priests due to their status as lower-level officials in the bureaucracy, while upper-level officials generally hold a hard line on organizational beliefs.

Priests also define PWAs primarily as terminally ill persons who are alienated from the church and stigmatized by society. Defining PWAs only as sick persons gives priests more flexibility in AIDS ministry, since they do not have to confront the issue of homosexuality. As a result, priests convey the love of God and the acceptance of the church toward PWAs.

Negotiating on the pastoral level and defining gay PWAs primarily as sick persons, as well as using the role-conflict strategies noted above, all help priests "get the job done" in their ministry. However, in order to achieve successful interactions with PWAs, priests have to build bridges between themselves as representatives of the church and PWAs by showing concern for them. In this way they hope to serve PWAs through their various ministerial roles over time. Yet PWAs do not always seek out priests as companions or counselors. These services are available to them from other sources, particularly through AIDS service agencies. Also, if PWAs are alienated from the church, it is likely that they will not go to a priest as their counselor of choice (see Veroff, Kulka, and Douvan 1981).[5]

Priests note that when they are called on to minister to PWAs, it is often at the last moment. They feel frustrated when they are asked to minister to a PWA who is dying but have not been sought as counselors. In such cases priests' status as religious professionals is not reinforced. Rather, the priests are seen by role partners as sacramental functionaries. While administering sacraments is important for priests, successful encounters with PWAs involve reconciling PWAs with the church and helping them cope psychologically with their illness. These successful experiences in ministry help reinforce priests' image of themselves as professionals and as representatives of the church. Successful encounters also enhance the church's public image as compassionate and conciliatory toward the sick without undermining either the magisterium or the ecclesiastical structure in which church teaching occurs.

6

Toward an Analysis of Ecclesiastical Organization

This study has examined how the Roman Catholic church has responded to the AIDS epidemic. The church's response to AIDS has provided a locus for examining power relationships within a normative organization. In addition, ways in which the organization attempts to maintain its survival and prestige in the modern world have been analyzed.

Church leaders, both bishops and priests, seek to fulfill the dual organizational goals of care for the sick and maintenance of church teaching despite the potential conflict between them. In part, church officials mediate any conflict in goals through an ecclesiastical division of labor whereby priests minister to PWAs as sick persons and bishops hold a hard line on church teaching. Yet this division of labor is not absolute. Bishops also call for compassionate treatment of PWAs, and priests see the need for upholding church teaching in the public context of AIDS education. Organizational officials also attempt to achieve their dual organizational goals through defining gay PWAs as sick persons rather than as gay men, and by emphasizing church teaching on sexuality in the public context of AIDS education while allowing for accommodation of church teaching on the private level of individual ministry.

I have noted the theological basis that allows church officials to minister to gay PWAs who possess a dual identity as sick persons and as "sinners." The church does not expect perfection in its members but sees all the faithful as traveling on a journey toward greater holiness. The church also teaches that the conscience of the individual is supreme and that pastoral ministers should respect the decisions of the well-formed conscience of the Christian. Thus, church officials can make concessions or accommodations in objective norms on the individual level. This theological understanding, however, provides for a church structure that allows for the limited autonomy of lower-level officials and laity, but only under the authority of higher-ranking clergy who hold formal organizational power.

I have noted that responses to AIDS from the Vatican have emphasized the church's official teaching on sexuality. The Vatican declaration on pastoral care to homosexual persons also defined the relationship of AIDS to homosexuality as the unfortunate deserts of "unnatural" sexual practices. Alternatively, AIDS might cause a shift toward a more open stance, or even a change in church teaching, with regard to homosexuality. The present study does not indicate that either of these responses to the AIDS crisis will characterize the church's general response to homosexuality in the future, although individuals and groups within the church will undoubtedly continue to advocate both of these positions. Indeed, the Vatican's stand toward homosexual persons appears to be increasingly conservative, as evidenced by the 1992 statement on the civil rights of homosexuals (see chapter 3).

Pastoral directives for PWAs coming from American bishops have emphasized the role of PWAs as sick persons while still proclaiming the church's official teaching. Church leaders encourage ministry to the sick and discourage the stigmatization of PWAs. Such a stance gives adequate flexibility to ministers and provides a route whereby the day-to-day work of pastoral ministry can continue while the hierarchical teachings of the organization remain uncompromised.

The response of the church to the AIDS crisis has provided an opportunity for priests to minister to PWAs without
condemning them. PWAs can receive reconciliation with the
church through its official representatives without having to
accept the church's official teaching on sexuality. Pastoral
concessions provide a door through which gay PWAs who
have left the church can find reconciliation and experience
the sacraments or receive other ministry from a priest,
should they desire such a reconciliation. While the church
does not need to publicly compromise official teaching,
PWAs may continue to voice opposition to official sexual
teachings and yet still receive acceptance through the
church's ministers because they are ill. For other gay PWAs,
reconciliation with the church may accompany a reconciliation with family members as well.

Thus, priests will continue to serve as intermediaries
for PWAs, both with a church from whom PWAs feel alienated and with families from which they are estranged. In this
way, priests have been able to accomplish the work of ministry while not publicly calling into question the church's
official teaching. This flexibility on the private level will continue in the church's response to AIDS. Yet pastoral accommodation should not be interpreted as a transformation in
official teaching on the issue of homosexuality.

As I have noted, the church's response to the AIDS crisis
has been influenced by the close links the disease has had
with homosexuality. Church leaders have distanced themselves from the issue of homosexuality by dealing with PWAs
in their role as sick persons, but not as gay men. As AIDS
moves out of the gay community, it will increasingly become
a disease significantly affecting other minority populations,
most notably poor African Americans and Hispanics. As this
trend continues, the church's ministry to PWAs will not be
hampered by the stigma of homosexuality. Rather, church
leaders may link their response to AIDS with their broader
"option for the poor." Nevertheless, the official church, given
its current teaching on sexual morality, cannot be expected

to publicly endorse AIDS prevention education even as a pastoral measure. Such endeavors will continue to be seen as a compromise on the official level with firmly entrenched moral absolutes. At the same time, such compromises may continue on the local level as long as they do not become publicized.

❧

PROFESSIONAL POWER AND INDIVIDUAL AUTONOMY

The limited flexibility of priests in ministry also adds to their self-understanding as religious professionals. Like other professionals, clergy see themselves as having authority to make decisions regarding pastoral "clients," even when such decisions may compromise the objective moral teaching of the church. The professionalization of the clergy can be seen as an attempt to heighten the prestige of the church in the modern world. Professionalization is another of the changes evident within post–Vatican II Catholicism. In fact, the clerical profession holds many similarities with other modern social service professions.

Wilding (1982) notes that social service professions hold power in policymaking and administration, define the needs and problems of their clients, have power over services provided to clients, have power over resource allocation, as well as control over defining the profession itself. As I have noted, not all members of the clergy exercise all the powers of the profession. Rather, there is a division of labor between upper and lower clergy with regard to the exercise of professional powers.

Friedson (1986) notes that a profession consists of administrators, practitioners, and teacher/researchers. In the context of Roman Catholic clergy, bishops act as administrators, and priests as practitioners. Theologians, who may not be ordained clergy, take on the role of teacher/researchers. They may be seen as part of the profession, however, in that they contribute to the profession's self-definition. Yet as Friedson maintains, teacher/researchers have no formal power in the profession, but their work may form the basis of administrative decisions. In the context of the church, the role of teacher is officially held by the pope and bishops, but theologians certainly contribute to the production of theological knowledge. Nevertheless, only the hierarchy controls what is considered official church teaching.

Administrators hold most of the organizational power, such as policymaking, regulation of the profession, control of resources, and power over practitioners. I have noted that the hierarchy holds formal control over both policy and the lower clergy. It is important to note also that hierarchical power over clergy practitioners includes control of financial remuneration, in that the bishop or religious superior, as a representative of the diocese or religious order, has control over the salaries of lower clergy and often may provide housing, food, clothing, and other necessities for practitioners.

Yet practitioners hold power over individual clients, attempt to define clients' needs, and have significant control over their own work. Additionally, as Friedson notes, clients also have a say in the services they receive from professionals. Indeed, I have demonstrated that bishops hold a hard line on the official teaching of the church while priests often make accommodations to the needs and beliefs of PWAs to whom they minister. This point also touches on the most interesting aspect of Friedson's work, the transformation of formal professional knowledge.

Friedson states that professional elites control the formal knowledge of the profession. For example, medical researchers, doctors, and so forth control knowledge considered "orthodox" within the medical profession. Administrators articulate the formal policies that make up the "discipline" of the profession. Friedson understands "discipline" in Foucault's (1977) sense—as both a segment of knowledge and the means by which that knowledge is applied to the affairs of others. Friedson states:

> Such disciplines establish the power of the norm, statis-
> tical or otherwise, which is used as a 'principle of coer-
> cion' in a variety of standardized institutions. (Friedson
> 1986, 6)

As I have noted, the Catholic hierarchy controls the discipline
of moral theology both in the production of formal, official
teaching and in attempting to define the actions of others in
response to that teaching. In this regard they attempt to manage the identity of the organization as well as the identities of
the adherents (see Cheney 1991). In the latter case, however,
priests play a more crucial role, since they are charged with
carrying out the bulk of ministry to the laity.

Within Catholicism the maintenance of professional
knowledge within the organization differs from that in many
other professions. Whereas in professions such as medicine
the evolution and growth of knowledge based on the scientific
method is exalted, such development is underplayed and even
denied within official Catholic teaching. Indeed, the hierarchy
defends a view of church teaching in which change does not
occur. Rather, knowledge is given to the church, and ecclesiastical professionals are charged with upholding the "deposit of
faith" and delivering it intact to the next generation.

Even so, Vatican II introduced the notion of the evolution of church teaching into the mainstream of official ecclesiastical discourse. It is this trend toward doctrinal development, along with a broader base in decision making, that
conservative church officials seek to neutralize.

Additionally, as Friedson notes, administrators within
many professions formulate procedures and substantive rules
based on the formal knowledge of the discipline. Practitioners
operate within the confines of organizational discipline but
often follow their own judgments even if these contradict the
official knowledge. Over time, such accommodation has the
ability to transform the official knowledge itself. I have demonstrated that the ability to accommodate official norms to the
contingencies of ministerial situations characterizes priests'

ministry to PWAs. Priests even use the official teaching on conscience to legitimate their concessions to PWAs' needs. Perhaps, in this regard, priests' experiences with individuals on the pastoral level may have the capacity to transform church teaching on sexuality over time. This study has demonstrated that while organizational administrators set official policy, such policy is then translated by practitioners into working knowledge so that they can implement organizational goals and "get the job done."

Given the fluidity of professional disciplines in allowing relative freedom of decision making for practitioners and clients, Friedson questions notions such as those of hegemony, social control, or monopoly of discourse, which have been used to characterize the control exercised by professional elites. These terms, Friedson argues, found in the work of such theorists as Foucault and Gramsci, assume that power elites of dominant social institutions exercise a high level of control over both professional knowledge and its application in the lives of lower level constituents. Such terms are overdrawn, take away from the reality of human autonomy, and give too much power to social institutions he argues. The power of disciplines or organizations over the lives of individuals, Friedson asserts, is not all-encompassing. Rather, professionals and clients, while working within the limits of the discipline, can exercise their own individuality and decision making. He argues:

> Knowledge cannot be treated as some fixed set of ideas or propositions organized into a discipline that is then employed mechanically by its agents. It lives only through its agents, who themselves employ ideas and techniques selectively as their tasks and perspectives dictate . . . knowledge is used selectively and transformed in the course of its use. (Friedson 1986, 217)

Both professionals and clients not only have control of the ways in which they apply the official teaching of the organization to their lives and work, but also play a part in the gradual transformation of knowledge. The fact that priests selectively use official teaching, and respect the moral decisions that PWAs make in conscience, supports Friedson's claims. Additionally, it must be emphasized that change occurs within church teaching over time based on pressures both inside and outside the church (Seidler 1986). A classic example is the change in the church's view on usury. Whereas in the Middle Ages lending money at interest was considered gravely sinful, in the modern era it is a common social practice virtually unquestioned by the church.

Despite the validity of Friedson's claims concerning the relative autonomy of both practitioners and clients in an organization, the present study has demonstrated that powerful social institutions limit the freedom of constituents and lower-level practitioners, as well as the official power they hold within the organization. Indeed, relative autonomy helps to maintain the structure of power within the organization. Local and ad hoc power gives an impression of autonomy while organizational elites continue to hold a monopoly on legitimate discourse within the institution. Accommodation on the pastoral level is secretive and tolerated within the organization, but does not represent structural change.

By focusing on the malleability of official knowledge, Friedson does not seriously analyze the power of organizational elites to control the transformation of discourse considered authoritative by the organization. This authority in the hands of the organizational leaders also controls the construction of the identity of the organization (Cheney 1991). In contrast, I have argued that local accommodation and relative autonomy are means that the organization can use to keep forces of change in check. The felt need for more substantive structural change is mitigated through limiting the dissatisfaction of constituents and lower-level officials.

In the case of the Roman Catholic church, I have noted the relative autonomy of lower clergy, but this must be seen in the context of the organizational power of the higher clergy to determine what and who is orthodox and who is heterodox or "deviant." Even though limited autonomy exists on the local level, and change in church teaching may occur over the course of several years or even centuries, and even though laity are involved in limited ways in Church decision making on the parish and diocesan levels and in some cases are consulted by the hierarchy on moral issues, the structure of authority remains unchanged and the laity still hold little real control in the institution.

APPARATUSES OF POWER

Power in social institutions can be understood only by examining its concrete expressions, beginning on the local level and in the whole web of relations of power in the institution (Foucault 1980a). In this regard, Foucault discusses "apparatuses of power" as the means by which power exists in the organization and is mediated on the local level. One of the most important of these apparatuses is the episteme (Foucault 1973, 1980a), that is, the content and methods by which legitimate discourse is generated.[1] In church teaching, and in the official moral theology of sexuality in particular, church officials have deduced moral norms from an "unchanging" natural law. This methodology has ensured a static notion of moral norms. Additionally, while the ecclesiastical episteme controls the production of legitimate theological discourse, control over who can have a voice in theological discourse itself becomes an apparatus of power.

Other apparatuses of power I have discussed include the variety of mechanisms for impression management existing within the institution, which co-opt dissent and limit dissatisfaction. Selznick (1948, 1966) states that organizations co-opt, or absorb, new elements into the leadership or policy structure of the organization to avert threats to its stability. Co-optation may be of two types. Formal co-optation takes representatives of interest groups or powerful individuals into the leadership of the institution, or provides formal vehicles for these groups to voice their concerns. This type of co-optation produces no real transferring of power, since the existing organizational elites still hold control. Conversely, informal co-optation occurs not through any formal channels, but on an ad hoc basis. Individuals or interest groups receive concessions from formal authority. These concessions do not receive wide publicity, since they may threaten the legitimacy of the organization.

Gramsci (1971) also notes the importance of compromises made with varying interest groups in order to maintain the hegemony of a power elite. Maintaining alliances with often disparate groups quells potential dissatisfaction (Bottomore et al. 1983). At the same time, the ruling elite seeks to cement its hegemony by emphasizing the values of allegiance to authority and faithfulness to tradition, thus cementing existing inequalities (Bocock 1986).

The ameliorative place of priests within the church organization serves to enhance organizational survival and prestige through informal co-optation of potential sources of critique. It is also important to note that formal co-optation has also occurred since Vatican II with the appearance of lay representatives on parish councils and other consultative groups. Yet these groups have little real power to affect decision making.

I have noted that by ministering to the needs of individual PWAs and gay persons in general on the local pastoral level, priests mollify this disenfranchised group and thus, perhaps unknowingly, co-opt dissent. As a result, potentially dissenting members have the impression that they have gained more power on the local level. In this way organizational clients are served, but power relations within the organization change very little.

Even on the local level, compromises do not often move beyond the controlled environment of the private counseling setting. Many priests who allow for more accommodation on the pastoral level recommend that such arrangements remain private and secretive. On the public level such clergy endorse the official teaching of the church. Priests who tolerate even less pluralism are more apt to emphasize official church teaching even on the pastoral level.

Yet local communities may create a more public image of the church that is dialogical and allows for accommodation in official church teaching. Acceptance of gay persons and of sexual relationships in the context of committed relationships exists in certain church-related groups such as Dignity or even in the parish-based groups for lesbians and gay men that exist in Los Angeles. Members of these local communities may perceive the church as a whole as accepting diversity on moral issues—though hierarchical attacks on these groups following the 1986 Vatican statement on the care of homosexual persons and the more recent statement on homosexual civil rights are likely to have shattered such illusions.

Limiting dissatisfaction is further achieved through the segmentation of personnel, an impression-management technique that I have discussed throughout this study. When higher-level clergy take a hard line on church teaching but lower-level practitioners have the ability to compromise within limits, the organization seeks to limit dissent from the Left and the Right. Liberal Catholics are presented with an image of the church as compromising, whereas conservative elements see that the official teaching remains the same. However, both sides also see the hierarchy's stand with the opposition, which produces limited dissatisfaction on both sides.[2]

Similarly, I have noted that even though the hierarchy clearly holds a hard line on church teaching in public statements, conciliation, dialogue, and compassion are emphasized, thereby deflecting attention away from church teaching on morality. In the context of AIDS ministry, the existence of diocesan hospices and masses for persons with AIDS creates an ecclesial image that accepts PWAs, but the question of church acceptance of the sexual orientation of gay PWAs is not emphasized. As a result, public dissent from official church views is lessened, as is conflict with church authority. At the same time, however, it should be noted that church members do in fact receive ministry through these forms of local accommodation, and their membership is retained within the organization.

Kennedy (1988) has noted the importance of pastoral concessions to the maintenance of hierarchical authority in the church. Kennedy has distinguished between two types of Catholicism, which he terms "Culture One" and "Culture Two." Culture One Catholicism is characterized by an institutional, hierarchical understanding of the church; whereas Culture Two is made up of Catholics not too concerned with the institution or what the hierarchy has to say. With reference to these two groups Kennedy writes:

> Indeed, many Culture One leaders realize that they compromise their own authority whenever they insist too much on laws that do not match the trustworthy life experience of Culture Two Catholics. Hence their emphasis on the pastoral approach in their dealings with them in recent years. (Kennedy 1988, 26)

Kennedy's comment is perceptive in that, as I have argued, church leaders co-opt potential dissent through the mechanism of the "pastoral approach." Culture Two Catholics may have more control over their own lives through pastoral concessions, and may have an impression that the church is more conciliatory, but this does not greatly damage the authority of the hierarchical elite in the institution.

In response, the large majority of Catholics will not feel a great desire to change church structures or leave the church, even though they may dissent on various church teachings. Seidler's (1979) concept of the church as a "lazy monopoly" is important in this regard. If the church can provide the minimal amount of satisfaction for its membership so that dissatisfaction is reduced to a bearable level, then substantive change will not occur within the structure in the short run. At the same time, those members who pressure for more change may leave the structure or be considered "deviants" on the fringe of the church who will not produce waves in the "critical mass" of the Catholic people. Over time, however, marginalized members' positions may become part of the official discourse. Indeed, the force of many small changes over time can bring about shifts in discourse such as occurred at Vatican II. Nevertheless, those empowered with creating such discourse remain the same dominant coalition within the organization.

Yet if the lower clergy and the people to whom they minister have relative power to make compromises in the official teaching, as I have maintained, does the hierarchy's monopoly on official discourse pose a significant threat to diversity in the church? I have argued, in the case of AIDS ministry, that priests and laity have achieved compromises in the official teaching. I have noted that such diversity at the local level may in fact bring about organizational change over time. Yet limited autonomy exercised on the local level by lower-level clergy and the laity helps maintain the status quo. Thus, the relative autonomy to make accommodations in church teaching on the local level is itself an apparatus of power in that the lower clergy and the laity are mollified by local experiences of autonomy and compromise. However, accommodation on the local level also allows for change within the organization over time. From the perspective of more traditional-minded Catholics, changes within church teaching that have already occurred have fundamentally altered Catholicism.

❦

CHANGE IN ORGANIZATIONAL STRUCTURES

❦

I have noted that criticism of church structures will be limited if dissenting lower-level clergy feel they have autonomy and can make accommodations in church teaching or pastoral directives in order to "get the job done" as religious professionals. Additionally, church authorities seek to limit dissatisfaction from the laity by managing impressions. Thus, hierarchical power remains relatively stable in the short run when (1) laypeople dissent from church teaching but perceive the official church as taking a stance of compromise, or (2) laypeople perceive the official church to be intransigent, but their particular experience of the church on the local level allows for compromises in official teaching. In short, the extent to which both lower-level clergy and laypeople criticize church structures is proportionate to the level in which they believe their religious needs are being met on the local level. Thus, organizational leaders seek to maintain the survival of the organization and preserve the status quo by limiting local dissatisfaction. Dominant coalitions are never totally successful, however. Innovation and transformation eventually occur over time through both endogenous and exogenous social variables affecting the organization.

Thus, the church is not a static entity. As I noted in chapter 1, the church, like other complex organizations, is an open system in the process of transformation. Seidler and Meyer (1989) maintain that no change occurs without conflict, and that the conflict already occurring in the church will eventually bring about changes in the structure. The presence of conflict reveals the church to be a dynamic rather than a static monolithic organization. Yet the present research indicates that Seidler and Meyer neglect the important elements of limited accommodation as neutralizing change occurring in ecclesiastical structures and indeed in complex organizations more generally.

As Thompson (1966) states, organizations seek to "buffer" what is considered the center or "core" of the organization's identity by negotiation at the organization's boundaries. I have demonstrated that limited organizational change, as well as negotiation with regard to the practical implementation of core teachings of the church, can itself be the buffer against more radical change, which conservative members of the organization's dominant coalition perceive as a threat to organizational survival. In other words, limited change is not only an accommodation to forces both inside and outside social organizations; it is also a means by which organizations actually inoculate themselves against further change threatening the organization's identity.

At the same time, however, the force of many small changes may bring about important large-scale change over time. The implementation of small changes before Vatican II, for example, led the way for the council. Yet the limited implementation of the structural changes initially conceived at Vatican II, I argue, can also be seen as an attempt to forestall further change. While there are implications for radical change in both the church's teaching and its structure implicit in the council documents, particularly concerning the evolution of church teaching, the priesthood of the laity, the "ministry" of the laity within the church, and the authority of conscience, these notions have received a more modest implementation in practice by organization leaders. Church teaching continues to be generated by the hierarchy and is proclaimed as immutable. The laity still have no real structural power within the organization. Yet the laity have their spiritual needs met on the local level and the hierarchy asserts that it is continuing to implement the changes called for at Vatican II.

While organizations undergo change and adaptation over time, dominant coalitions seek to maintain the stability of the organization. Too little change prevents the organization from effectively interfacing with its environment, but dominant coalitions preserve the organization from too much change. Such coalitions seek to preserve the unique and distinctive characteristics of the organization so that it does not simply blend into the rest of the society. The church, facing the modern world, is an organization that has a special stake in preserving its distinctive character.

Indeed, it is part of the organization's charter to keep alive the faith of the apostles. Too much change may cause as much or more defection from the organization as too little change, in that members may see little difference in remaining Catholic or participating in another religious body or in none at all. Ebaugh (1977) notes the problems caused by the changes of Vatican II for religious orders within the church. Although changes were implemented to make religious life more attractive to young people, there was also a lessening of the distinctiveness of such a vocation and the sense of solidarity shared by group members. Orders that implemented the changes of Vatican II most strongly were the very ones that experienced the greatest loss of members. A similar situation occurred in the church as a whole. As I note in chapter 1, the changes effected by Vatican II caused a legitimation crisis within an organization that highlighted its unchangeableness. The distinctiveness of being a Catholic in the preconciliar church served as a benefit worth the costs imposed upon members. Catholics ever since the council have attempted to reevaluate the distinctive features of Catholicism. Organizational leaders, especially during the pontificate of John Paul II, have attempted return to a preconciliar Catholicism in order to rescue its distinctiveness, but such a return is unlikely to occur. Despite attempts by organizational leadership to preserve the status quo, forces of change continue to exist within the church. A great deal of conflict continues to surround the question of what constitutes the core of the Catholic tradition and what makes Catholicism distinctive, such as the debate over dissent on noninfallible church teachings; but this is a question far beyond the scope of the present work.

7

Toward a Normative Critique of Church Structures

Discourse transmits and produces power; it reinforces it but also undermines and exposes it, renders it fragile and makes it possible to thwart it. In like manner, silence and secrecy are a shelter for power, anchoring its prohibitions; but they also loosen its holds and provide for relatively obscure areas of tolerance.

—*Michel Foucault*

In previous chapters I have discussed Catholic clergy responses to the AIDS crisis. I have also examined how such responses reflect larger issues of authority and change within the structure of the Catholic church. In this chapter, I will present a normative analysis of the priest-counselor's role as the church's representative and minister to the faithful. Additionally, I will discuss the broader issues of power within the church structure, as well as changes in church teaching and structure from a normative perspective. However, I do so as one who now stands outside the Roman Catholic church.

Priests as Ministers and Mediators

One area in which priests in this study expressed unanimity was in their belief that PWAs should be treated with the compassion of Christ. Yet, regarding their ministry to PWAs, priests expressed differing ideas concerning how they related their ministry on the pastoral, subjective level with the objective teaching of the church regarding sexuality. These differences are based on two ways of understanding church teaching, which I discussed in chapter 1. The first sees church teachings on moral issues, part of the "ordinary magisterium," as fixed and changeless norms. Yet individuals may fall short of the norm. Although the "sin" is objectively wrong, the sinner receives the compassion of Christ. From this perspective, all Christians are sinners on the journey toward perfection. The second view is more open to dissent from official teaching on moral issues, if the individual dissents from a particular teaching in conscience. The conscience of the dissenter must be informed by the church's teaching, which the dissenter must regard seriously before dissenting from it.

With regard to the first position, the most conservative priests I studied, while noting the need for compassion toward the sick, believed that if a PWA did not uphold the magisterium's view on sexuality as an ideal, he could not be fully reconciled with the church. There was no room for a plurality of positions within the church. Still, if a PWA accepted the teaching of the magisterium as an ideal, albeit one that was difficult to achieve, then he could be reconciled with the church.

A related point concerns the distinction between objective norms and the lack of subjective culpability. Many priests still upheld magisterial teaching as the ideal but allowed for the presence of impediments that might keep the individual from living out the church's teaching. In this way, gay PWAs might be reconciled with the church even though they did not live up to it. They would not be culpable for violating the norms of the church's sexual teaching, because of the presence of circumstances in their lives that would impede them from living out the norm. As I note in chapter 1, the individual in such a case is in a state of "invincible ignorance" of the norm due to these impediments and thus should receive special pastoral consideration. In the case of gay persons, sexual orientation itself may present an impediment to carrying out the church's moral norms, placing the individual in a state of invincible ignorance for which he or she should receive special pastoral concern and sensitivity. From this perspective, however, the norm itself is not open for dialogue.

In the second perspective priests accept the position of dissent made from a well-formed conscience. Once these priests explained the church's teaching, the individual to whom the priest ministered had the opportunity to dissent and still receive reconciliation with the church. From this perspective, the church's ministers should assist the faithful in developing their own consciences so that they may make proper moral decisions affecting their lives, as long as such a position is theologically probable.[1]

The first perspective, which firmly upholds the church's magisterium as the unchanging norm, gives power for ethical decision making to the church hierarchy, with little input from the person to whom the priest ministers. Such pastoral relationships are characterized not by dialogue, but rather by the acceptance or rejection of an unchanging absolute. While pastoral accommodations can be made for specific cases, the individual is made to realize that anything that falls short of the church's sexual norms is deviant. This position reflects the dominant view of the majority of the hierarchy, particularly Pope John Paul II.

The second position admits more dialogue in the pastoral encounter. While church teaching is given varying degrees of importance by different priests, the pastoral minister enters the encounter with more willingness to hear the life story of the individual Christian with whom he is ministering. The experience of the individual has a more prominent place in the dialogical encounter between the priest and the individual to whom he ministers. As I will discuss more fully below, this perspective allows for more input on the part of the laity. Indeed, both positions outlined above reflect larger issues of authority and teaching within the church as a whole.

❦

ROMA LOCUTA, CAUSA FINITA, OR SENSUS FIDELIUM?

The traditional hierarchical authority of the church, as well as traditional church teachings, have increasingly been criticized by Catholic laity and even many clergy since the Second Vatican Council. What is at issue is a conflict between two epistemes. The first episteme is the traditional one that I have discussed at length in this study, the one that has held a monopoly of discourse in the church both before and after the Second Vatican Council. Having power over the production and content of "orthodox" knowledge in the church, it has operated as a "unitary discourse" (Foucault 1980a, 86). The motto of this traditional paradigm has been "Roma locuta, causa finita" (Rome has spoken, the matter is settled)—a phrase that sums up the attempts of church leaders to silence all plurality of positions in favor of the dominant theological voice.

I have noted that Vatican II made significant changes in the church and represented the primary institutional attempt of Catholicism to adapt to the modern world. Indeed, although prepared for by years of conflict both inside and outside the church, Vatican II can be seen as an epistemic break in Catholic theological discourse. It provided the point from which a new episteme could take shape. Yet theologians in the postconciliar period have attempted to define the boundaries of theological discourse, and moral theology in particular, within a new episteme. What shape should moral theological discourse take in the postconciliar church? The postconciliar episteme has emphasized two key issues: (1) that Vatican II paved the way for the voice of the laity to be part of the church's moral discourse, and (2) that historically there has been a development of church teaching over time, despite the ideological assertion that magisterial teaching is immutable.

The notion of the *sensus fidelium* (the discernment or sense of the faithful) emphasized in the documents of Vatican II, particularly *Lumen Gentium*, provides a fruitful starting point for a more inclusive moral theology. Not only does this concept incorporate the voices of bishops as decision makers, but the whole people of God have a voice in the church's discourse (see Abbott 1966, 29–30). The laity have a right to express their views within the church and to apply the church's teaching according to their conscience. In doing so, they are led by the Spirit not only through their reason, but also by the intuition they are given through the Spirit's prompting (Mahoney 1987, 207–8).

That the laity is led by the inner witness of the Holy Spirit presents the church with a challenge to listen to the voices that have not been heard in the church's discourse. In the context of the present study, this applies particularly to gay persons, but it also refers to the voices of women, persons of color, and other disenfranchised groups. The realization that groups of marginalized laity are led by the Spirit and have a voice in theological discourse has set the stage for what Foucault (1980a, 81) might term an "insurrection of subjugated knowledges" (see also Welch 1985).

Foucault defines "subjugated knowledges" in two ways. First, they are those blocs of knowledge that have been part of the dominant tradition but have laid dormant and have been masked by the dominant discourse. Second, they consist of knowledge that has been discounted or disqualified as low-ranking or naive. Yet it is not only certain forms of knowledge or discourse that are marginalized by the dominant tradition, but rather groups of persons have been marginalized and excluded from the production of knowledge by those who have upheld the unitary discourse, the professional elites, who, within the church, have consisted of the hierarchy and to a lesser extent professional theologians to the degree that they have acted in the interests of the ruling hierarchy.

Foucault (1980a, 82) calls the discourse produced by these marginalized factions "le savoir des gens" (popular knowledge). In the Catholic context such popular discourse would be found in the lived experience of the people of God—particularly those subgroups of laity noted above. Foucault notes that when subjugated knowledges are introduced into the broader discourse they produce conflict. Because such conflict can bring about change, Foucault cautions that as soon as these subjugated knowledges appear within the field of the unitary discourse, they run the risk of "recolonization" by the dominant episteme and thus lose their critical edge. It is important to note, however, that Foucault does not deny that change occurs within the discourse or that subjugated knowledges have a role in the production of change. Yet he does make clear that the dominant discourse presents itself as unitary and appropriates changes in order to maintain its power.

The question remains, though, concerning the appropriate role for voices of subjugated groups within the church. Sharon Welch (1985) has appropriated Foucault's critique of dominant discourses and applied it to a feminist Christian theology. Her perspective deserves consideration for theological discourse within the Catholic tradition. Welch notes the importance of communities of resistance and solidarity; that is, faith communities that "remember" strands of the Christian tradition long forgotten or submerged. Borrowing from Metz (1980), Welch refers to these strands of tradition as "dangerous memories." Such memories include a liberational understanding of the Exodus story or the promises of justice in the future reign of God from the gospels. Welch states:

> The memory is of a community in which people were freed to claim an identity different from that imposed on them. It is both a memory of past liberation and a motivation for further liberation. It is a memory of resistance and of hope for further resistance. (Welch 1985, 42)

These liberational memories become a point from which marginalized communities can create their own identities. They become places where marginalized persons can articulate their own faith experiences. They are places in which the *savoir des gens* is given voice.

Furthermore, communities of those at the fringes of church and society, out of their own experience of exclusion and marginalization, can in a limited way understand the marginalization of others and through this understanding weave a web of solidarity with them. Such communities are also based in the praxis of working in the present to end the oppression of the marginalized through working for the establishment of more inclusive and just social structures in society and in the church.

Welch's perspective allows for the voicing of views not often heard in theological discourse. Discourse emerging from such marginalized communities should be privileged, she notes. Yet she sees the experience and reflection of such alternative discourse communities as being normative theological reflections in themselves. There is no role for the judgment of the hierarchy in the articulation of moral teaching as it concerns subjugated groups. Since the hierarchical teaching office is integral to Roman Catholic self-understanding, Welch's position must be modified to include not only the perspective of the oppressed, but that of the hierarchy as well.

While the *savoir des gens* needs to reshape a Catholic notion of the *sensus fidelium*, it is not sufficient in itself. The moral discourse of subjugated groups does not make up the whole sense of the faithful. A Catholic understanding of the *sensus fidelium* needs to include those who have traditionally been marginalized as well as all the laity in union with the bishops and the pope. In the end, the hierarchy, as the church's official teachers, has the duty to articulate the church's moral teaching. Yet this does not mean a return to authoritarian Catholicism. Even after such teaching has been articulated, subjugated groups of laity in the church have a voice. Yet the role of articulating church teaching remains part of the episcopal and petrine ministries in the church.

❧

RECEPTION AND CHURCH TEACHING

I have noted that the hierarchy, especially at higher levels within the organization, has emphasized church teaching as absolute and immutable while veiling the development of church teaching over time clearly present in the church's history.[2] Additionally, church leaders present an image of a unitary discourse that has not been influenced by the discourse of the people of God. Yet the new episteme emergent in the church since Vatican II has embraced a historical consciousness. There has in fact been a tradition of change in church teaching in response to dissenting voices, and this has existed throughout church history, but the dominant discourse has not acknowledged the role of dissent in the development of teaching.

Congar's notion of "reception" is relevant to a discussion of the development of church teaching, as well as to an understanding of who participates in the production of discourse in the church.[3] Congar notes that in the history of the church there has always been a sense in which church teaching has been received by the people of God. Such reception is not that of obedience, in the sense that one receives a command and carries it out. Rather,

> it includes a degree of consent, and possibly of judgment, in which the life of a body is expressed which brings into play its own original spiritual resources. (Congar 1972, 45)

Thus, the notion of reception is a dialogical concept in which not only church teaching is given to the people of God, but they interact with it and give their consent. Congar notes that this may be a "dangerous theme" in Catholic ecclesiology; at the least it is one that has received little attention from the hierarchy. Congar notes that the concept of reception as he defines it is excluded from discourse when there exists

> a wholly pyramidal conception of the church as a mass totally determined by its summit, in which . . . there is hardly any mention of the Holy Spirit other than as the guarantor of an infallibility of hierarchical courts, and where the conciliar decrees themselves become papal decrees. (Congar 1972, 60)

Congar counters this model of the church with one in which the faithful have a voice, or, better, the whole ecclesia takes part in discerning and receiving the teaching of the church.

At the same time, as King (1977) maintains, the notion of reception should not be seen simply as a frequently used veto power over church teaching. Church leaders should look to the receptivity of the people of God concerning a particular teaching before promulgating it. Even after teachings are in place, however, "nonreception" may occur. Church leaders should view nonreception not as recalcitrance, King continues, but as a contribution to the legislative process in the church by the Christian community.

An example of the reversal of church teaching through a lack of reception can be found in the church's stance on religious freedom (Dionne 1987). Pius IX gave little room for religious freedom by upholding the unity of church and state. Yet rejection by the rest of the church gradually led to a change and a reversal in the papal position, as seen in the Decree on Religious Liberty promulgated by the Second Vatican Council. Dionne notes that initially those who dissented from the papal position, such as John Courtney Murray, were in the minority. Yet responsible "talking back" led to a later change in teaching.

As Dionne notes, tension between the hierarchy and other factions within the church can be a healthy sign of the movement of the Holy Spirit within the church. Yet the official church has failed to admit the innovation in doctrine that became part of church teaching as the result of reception. Dionne concludes that the hierarchy needs to recognize the dynamic of change through conflict that has historically existed within the church, and that participants in this more collegial notion of reception need to include the hierarchy, the laity, and the entire people of God.

Like Boff (1985), Dionne calls for a renewed understanding of the *ecclesia discens* and the *ecclesia docens*. In the dominant episteme, the laity made up the *ecclesia discens*, or that element of the church taught by the hierarchy, and the hierarchy existed as *ecclesia docens*, or the teaching church. This strict division of roles, however, is theologically unsound. The whole church is taught by the Holy Spirit, and both the hierarchy and the laity teach within the *ecclesia*. As Boff contends:

> *docens* and *discens* are two aspects of the one community; they are two adjectives that describe two practices of the whole community. They are not two nouns that split the community. . . . there is mutual teaching within the church . . . the hierarchy becomes a member of the *Ecclesia discens* and the laity becomes a member of the *Ecclesia docens*.(Boff 1985, 139)

In the paradigm of the church put forth by Boff, there is a mutuality of decision making within the church structure. There is a place for the laity as well as the hierarchy to become involved in church teaching.

Since the Holy Spirit is the principle teacher of the whole church, and since the Spirit speaks to the whole people of God, especially through concrete experiences in the world, the laity have a role to play in the church's teaching on moral issues. There is a dialogue between the clergy and the people that should be open and accepted within the church's structure; that is, a mutual reception of teaching by the hierarchy, the laity, and theologians.

A question that may be presented at this point is how this dialogue exists, or, better, should exist, in the church. To a certain extent, the dialogical nature of pastoral encounters often allows for the experience of particular laypersons to interface with official church teaching.[4] Laypeople, in dialogue with the priest as representative of the whole community, receive the church's teaching or do not receive it. Nonreception, after consideration of the official teaching, can be an important statement to the church as a whole, especially if a large number of the laity do not receive the official teaching. Perhaps the whole body of the faithful need to reconsider a particular teaching when many in the community do not receive it.

Additionally, as King notes, a teaching may be received by many in the church, but it may fail to take into account certain sociocultural conditions or certain groups within the whole church for whom a particular teaching may be inappropriate. King implies that there is a possibility for a plurality of positions within the same church. For example, in the context of my study, the church's teaching on the importance of procreation in sex may be appropriate for certain groups within the church, but the gay community sees this view as not a necessary component of Christian expressions of committed sexual love between persons. Indeed the whole emphasis on procreation as integral to loving sexual expressions needs reexamination not simply by the hierarchy and theologians, but by the whole people of God. The local pastoral context is perhaps the best place for dialogue on such issues to occur, since the pastoral setting is the nexus where both the laity and the clergy meet.

While theologians who espouse a model of reception often note that it has historically been the mode by which church teaching develops, despite the hierarchy's reluctance to acknowledge this point, the historical examples reception theologians cite often do not include a widespread integration of the perspective of lay people in the development of teaching. Rather, examples of reception more often deal with the eventual recognition of a view held by dissenting theologians and clergy, but rarely by the laity, particularly marginalized laity.

Even in the decades after Vatican II, structural barriers continue to prevent marginalized groups of laity from participating fully in the dominant discourse. The implementation of dialogue between church leaders, theologians, and social scientists has also been thwarted. The dominant episteme continues to control hierarchical decisions concerning church teaching with little input from other sources.

In short, reception theologians have articulated an important point with regard to the dialogical nature of moral teaching. Additionally, they give respect to the hierarchy's ministry of teaching and the role the laity should have in receiving such teaching. However, reception theologians generally do not highlight the importance of the voice of traditionally marginalized groups of laity in the church's discourse. Additionally the hierarchy has not fully embraced the notion of reception. In the years since Vatican II, the laity still have not received an adequate hearing in the church's moral discourse, nor has dissent been an acceptable response to church teaching. While the hierarchy needs to be respected as official teachers within the church, the importance of the voices of the marginalized as well as the acceptance of nonreception in the church must also be given priority.

❦

POWER AND KNOWLEDGE: FURTHER EXAMPLES

❦

I have discussed the power of the dominant ecclesiastical paradigm as it has appeared in the response of the church to the AIDS epidemic. These apparatuses of power operate also in other responses of the church to issues involving sexual morality, such as official Vatican teaching on contraception. Additionally, even the American hierarchy, in its statements on social issues, has largely continued in the traditional episteme, although it has created an impression of implementing a more dialogical paradigm far greater than any change in the structure of church teaching itself. This is, of course, not to say that such change has been unimportant, but it is not sufficient.

Humanae Vitae

I have commented on the traditional episteme clearly expressed in the 1986 Vatican letter on homosexuality. Such a view, however, is evident in all official Roman Catholic sexual teaching. In the papal encyclical *Humanae Vitae*, for example, Paul VI, quoting the Second Vatican Council's document *Gaudium et Spes*, states:

> Marriage and conjugal love are by their nature ordained toward the begetting and educating of children. Children are really the supreme gift of marriage and contribute very substantially to the welfare of their parents. (Paul VI 1968)

Given this "natural" order, the pope concludes:

> The church, calling men [*sic*] back to the observance of the norms of the natural law, as interpreted by her constant doctrine, teaches that each and every marriage act . . . must remain open to the transmission of life.

This norm is clearly in line with previous Vatican teaching on sexual acts in marriage.[5] It admits no possibility of the moral use of contraceptives or the morality of any sexual act outside of marriage.

As I have noted, there can be pastoral concessions for those individuals who do not live up to the norm, but the norms themselves, in this episteme, are said not to change or evolve, despite historical evidence to the contrary. The pontiff notes the role that the laity play in receiving the church's teaching, but he sees such reception as assent to the papal magisterium. Clearly, the group that has a voice in moral discourse remains the same, that is, the pope and bishops, with little constructive input from those laity who are affected by the document.

When the pope discusses pastoral directives, he states that the official teaching can be accommodated to pastoral situations. This is true in the sense that individuals only gradually live out the Christian life in its fullness. Nevertheless, as Seidler and Meyer (1989)[6] point out, the promulgation of *Humanae Vitae* brought a great deal of dissatisfaction from American Catholics who, inspired by the spirit of the council, expected a change in the traditional teaching on birth control. Many Catholics, including theologians and some bishops, looked for the implementation of a more empirically based theology that looked to the experience of the people of God rather than simply relying on deductive principles.

On the pastoral level, since the late 1960s, priests have made concessions in applying the official teaching on contraception to individual situations. Many Catholics do not attribute their use of artificial birth control to human weakness, but simply disagree with the norm itself. As Gallup and Castelli (1987, 183) note, dissent on church teaching against contraception has been on the rise since Vatican II. Three Catholics in four believe that one can practice birth control and still be a good Catholic. Yet if these Catholics can remain part of the community, receiving pastoral accommodations on the local level while holding views that diverge from official teaching, they will not be a disruptive force for the church, at least in the short run. At the same time, church leaders will not view dissent on this issue as an act of nonreception by the people of God. Dissent on the issue of contraception has brought about not creative dialogue, but rather continued reassertions of the papal teaching.

What is also noteworthy about *Humanae Vitae* is the manner in which the document was written. Pope Paul VI, attempting to implement the changes of Vatican II, established a commission to advise him on this encyclical. The commission examined the findings of social science, as well as the reflections of modern theologians on the contraception issue. When the commission recommended views on contraception that did not support the traditional teaching of the church, the pontiff disregarded their findings in favor of the document as it now stands. Thus, the development of *Humanae Vitae* further demonstrates how the hierarchical elites attempt to present an impression of accommodation to the modern world, as well as of implementing a consultative methodology, yet quickly discard such reforms when they affect "immutable" hierarchical teaching. Additionally, the ease with which the pontiff disregarded the commission's report reveals that no real power had shifted hands. While the pope has the duty to articulate church teaching, Paul VI still pronounced church teaching from the traditional paradigm.

The U.S. Bishops' Pastoral Letters

In the United States, further examples of a "dialogical" and "consultative" methodology in church teaching are important to discuss. The most notable examples include the American Catholic bishops' letters *The Challenge of Peace: God's Promise and Our Response* (United States Catholic Conference of Bishops 1983), which dealt at length with the nuclear arms race, and *Economic Justice for All: Catholic Social Teaching and the U.S. Economy* (United States Catholic Conference of Bishops 1985). Both of these documents dealt with the church's social teaching rather than sexual issues. This is not surprising, given that even papal social teaching has made use of a more progressive methodology when dealing with social issues. Curran (1982, 185) comments that Catholic social teaching, particularly after Vatican II, has its basis in a human anthropology that "stresses freedom, equality, participation and historical mindedness." Curran continues:

> Gone is the vision of a universal plan deductively
> derived from natural law and proposed authoritatively
> by the church magisterium to be applied in all parts of
> the world. (Curran 1982, 189)

Despite this shift, Pope John Paul II is more comfortable with
reinvigorating Catholic social doctrine universally applied
within the church (see Hebblethwaite 1983). Nevertheless,
the American bishops are on safer ground using a methodology in dialogue with the social sciences, theologians, and
laypeople when discussing social issues than when they discuss sexual morality—an area in which church teaching has
not experienced a similar progressive turn. Yet even these
documents give evidence of hierarchical impression management.

The American bishops made use of a more empirically
based, dialogical, and consultative methodology in writing
both of these pastoral letters. When developing the pastoral
letter on the economy, for example, the drafting committee
worked for over two years, hearing from theologians, histo-
rians, economists, people who worked with the poor, and
leaders of various other Christian denominations. The bishops prepared a draft of the letter in 1984 and invited
responses from the American public and the Catholic laity
before the bishops voted on a final draft in November 1985.

While this process goes far in developing a broader
base for the development of church social teaching, those
who were invited to make comments on the letter were
largely theologians and other professionals. Citing the pastoral letter on the U.S. economy as an example once again,
few voices of the poor themselves were heard in the bishops'
deliberations. This fact was noted by Archbishop Rembert
Weakland, one of the chief architects of the document (see
Blush 1985). Moreover, the first part of the letter, articulating the bishops' basic principles, is based primarily on previous magisterial teaching. The bishops make use of few
empirical or theological insights they have garnered from

their dialogue. Rather, the bishops maintain the older hierarchical methodology. While part 2 of the document makes use of insights gained through dialogue, these ideas are largely descriptive or refer to tentative recommendations for change in American economic life. Thus, the impression of dialogue and the democratization of church teaching in the pastoral letter is greater than the actual impact of a dialogical methodology on the content of the document.

The Moral Voice of Catholic Laity

If conflict is the stuff of which change is made, then it is important to keep a critical edge to the discourse of disenfranchised groups in spite of limited accommodation. It is far easier to be satisfied with an all-too-facile accommodation on the local level than to oppose the continued and increasing reemergence of the dominant episteme in the larger church structure. Yet this fact does not imply that those concerned with changing church structures must eliminate pluralism on the local level to heighten tension among the disenfranchised.

Fundamental to the task of developing new structures is the unmasking of current structures when they appear to be open to change but in reality resist it. The goal of my study has been to reveal ecclesial structures that seem to be accommodating and conciliatory but that tend to perpetuate the dominant episteme. Yet I believe that the very diversity on the local level, which in one sense has brought about a quietistic response to the dominance of the preconciliar episteme, may also be the vehicle by which change occurs.

In the short run, ecclesiastical impression management may be effective in bringing stability to the organization, but it will be ineffective in the long run. First, although assenting to the conscience of the laity on the individual level can bring about personal quietism with regard to church structures, the post–Vatican II emphasis on the voice of the laity in moral issues has questioned the authority of the hierarchy to simply dictate moral norms without a sufficient hearing from those affected by the church's moral teaching. Second, while local communities that dissent from official teaching can create an insulated environment not highly critical of the hierarchical episteme, these communities have the potential to provide conflict within the organization and to bring about constructive change through voicing their dissent. Again, such dissent must be based on decisions of a well-formed conscience; that is, a conscience informed by the teaching of the church.

The continued conscientization of marginalized groups of laypeople may bring about a further democratization of church structures. That is, the more disenfranchised laypeople become empowered with a sense of their role as baptized believers led by the Spirit, the more they will press for a greater voice in the church. Nevertheless, democratization should not be understood simply as "one person, one vote." Rather, as noted above, the episcopal office still has a role in articulating church teaching, but this must be informed by a consistent and continuing dialogue with groups of laity affected by such teaching.

The postconciliar church in the United States has already seen the emergence of personal agency and the moral maturing of American Catholics. Many Catholics dissent from the magisterium and in some cases even leave the church. Many priests, indeed the priests sampled for my study, acknowledged that Catholic people need to be taught to be mature believers. They asserted the need for Catholics to be less dependent on authority figures for their moral decision making. Perhaps this very teaching, inspired by Vatican II, has helped to bring about the greater autonomy found among American Catholics since the council.

American Catholics are more willing to make moral decisions based on their own conscience than were their fathers and mothers a generation ago, particularly with regard to sexual issues. As Gallup and Castelli (1987) conclude:

> The Catholic church . . . has lost its credibility on everything related to sex. American Catholics do not disregard church teaching on every issue, but birth control clearly established the pattern that they accept church teaching only when it makes sense in terms of their own situations and their own consciences. When it comes to sex, church leaders are preaching to an audience that is simply not paying any attention. Preaching more loudly or more often or in more sympathetic tones will not change that.

Gallup and Castelli's findings do not bode well for the fate of institutional church teaching or the hierarchical authority structure in the long run.

The autonomy and freedom of conscience experienced by many Catholics is at odds with the tone set by the majority of the hierarchy. As Deedy (1987) reports, American bishops have followed the conservative lead of Rome and have expressed an unswerving deference to Vatican authority. This study has shown that the American Catholic bishops in their response to AIDS have attempted to steer a middle course, manage impressions, and maintain the stability of the organization. Despite the American hierarchy's attempt to quiet dissatisfied factions within the church, the renewed assertion of the hierarchical episteme, coming especially from the Vatican, will generate continued conflict and resistance from grassroots Catholics.

American Catholics want to have a voice in the moral decisions that affect their lives, but they are not finding a conversation partner in the institutional church. If church leaders would open the church's moral discourse and encourage marginalized laity to voice their views, based on their experience, church teaching could have a larger role in shaping the moral decisions of traditionally disenfranchised lay Catholics. At the same time, if church leaders engaged in careful and respectful listening, and were open to the possibility of change, church teaching itself would be shaped through the influence of the laity. The more the hierarchy clings to a preconciliar paradigm for moral theology, the less influence they will have on the moral decisions of marginalized lay Catholics.

AIDS, the Gay Community, and the Church

I return now to a discussion of the particular marginalized community I have focused on in this study—gay Catholics in the midst of the AIDS crisis. The ministry of gay-affirming priests, on the local level, is important to the reintegration of PWAs into the community of the church—a community from which they have often felt alienated and marginalized. Such reintegration can be a source of spiritual healing for those suffering from terminal illness. Priests report that gay men who have contracted AIDS have returned to find reconciliation with the church, and often on the terms PWAs desire. On the local level, many priests have been willing to make these compromises, but many times the reconciliation has simply been a sacramental one. While gay PWAs may find representatives of the church who are willing to compromise official teaching, any reconciliation they receive is still secretive.

Moreover, the hierarchy has attempted to curtail the open public dissent of gay men in the church through attacks on organizations such as Dignity. This is why gay men who wish to remain within the church cannot simply accept the facile reconciliation the church offers them on the pastoral level. Gays and lesbians need to publicly challenge the church's opposition in efforts to create conflict and to perhaps evoke more change. At the same time they are able to join the broader critique of church structures such as that advanced by women in the church. As Harrison states:

> It is precisely [gay] men who are often able to hear a
> feminist analysis of sexuality and who join us in making

the connections between homophobia and misogyny. What generates rage against gay men is that, by coming out, they signal that they will no longer cooperate in refusing to rock the ecclesiastical boat: they join women in expecting the church, finally, to come of age regarding human sexuality. (Harrison 1985, 143–44)

It is the openness to critique and a rejection of secretive accommodation that enrages church officials and brings about conflict.

Conflicts between the gay and lesbian community and the official church have mounted in the face of perceived inadequacy of official church responses to the AIDS crisis and Vatican attacks on homosexuality. Many bishops in the United States, for example, have withdrawn support for Dignity and have even forbidden priests to celebrate the Eucharist for the group. Dignity has issued a public statement rejecting the official church teaching on homosexuality and calling gay sexuality a "holy gift of God" (Los Angeles Times, 16 September 1989). A public rejection of the secretive pastoral accommodations put forward by the church structure has engendered rage in the hierarchy against Dignity and gay Catholics in general.

Many gays and lesbians have left the church, in part because their experience of their sexuality does not fit officially prescribed moral norms. This strategy can be a prophetic protest from outside the institution. Yet exiting helps to maintain the church structure as a "lazy monopoly" (Seidler 1979; Seidler and Meyer 1989) wherein only those who are satisfied with minimal service remain within the structure. At the same time, a gay-affirming critique of the official church cannot be directed simply at symptoms of the larger problem (e.g., criticizing the refusal of the official church to solemnize gay unions). Rather, it needs to confront the very structures of moral discourse, in which an ecclesiastical elite holds control over the means of religious production (see Maduro 1982; Boff 1985) while those affected by church teaching have no voice.

Substantive ecclesiastical change can occur only through

opening of the church's moral discourse so that those affected by official church teaching have a voice in its production. Yet these alternative voices will not find expression in the institutional church unless they first speak through the alternative discourse of local communities who join in solidarity with the socially and ecclesiastically disenfranchised. The experience of solidarity and personal empowerment found in such communities has the potential to become the basis of resistance toward institutional oppression, and the source of critical reflection for a broader theology of liberation.

Further implications of this study need more examination than I have been able to offer here. How can marginalized laity, and laity in general, gain a voice in the church's moral discourse while still respecting the role of the petrine and episcopal ministries in church teaching? What is the relationship of plural moral positions to the Great Tradition, or the teaching of the church as a whole? These are some of the important theological questions my study has raised. Although it may be difficult to integrate the hierarchical teaching office with the perspectives of subjugated knowledges, to do so is necessary within the current Catholic understanding of the church. Further work is necessary to answer these questions as part of the movement of theological discourse toward the inclusion of the whole people of God.

NOTES

Chapter 1. Introduction

1. Dingwall and Strong note that an organization's official charter is articulated not only in its official documents, but in its day-to-day working and its official public events.

2. While the official Roman Catholic view on sexual morality views sexuality as a gift from God, sexual acts are licit only in the context of heterosexual monogamous marriage open to the possibility of procreation. Thus, extramarital or premarital sexual acts between heterosexuals, and all homosexual acts even within a committed relationship, are illicit. Even sexual acts between a married couple who use contraceptives are considered illicit since they attempt to thwart the procreative function of sex. The American Catholic bishops (National Conference of Catholic Bishops [NCCB] 1976, 19) in discussing homosexuality state that while homosexual acts are wrong, homosexual persons deserve basic human rights and deserve pastoral consideration since they can never look forward to marriage. A more recent Vatican statement (Sacred Congregation for the Doctrine of Faith 1986) took a harder line on church teaching and stated that homosexuals themselves are intrinsically disordered, while noting that although homosexuals deserve the dignity accorded to all persons, civil rights should be denied them (see secs. 7, 9, 11).

3. In his discussion of rational-legal authority, Weber (1947, 334) mentions the structure of the Roman Catholic church as an example of bureaucratic administration. Yet the church's authority is legitimated by traditional means.

4. Maduro speaks at length in the beginning of *Religion and Social Conflicts* about a myopic view of religion informed only by one's own experience. However, his analysis of intrareligious conflict seems to reflect the Catholic reality more than other religious traditions. Even among Western

religions, his analysis of "higher" and "lower" clergy, for example, would not fit in a Jewish context, or even within the polity of many Protestant bodies. The same could be said of his strict separation between clergy and laity.

5. As Wilding (1982) notes, the term *professional* has its roots in the profession of vows made by Roman Catholic clergy in the Middle Ages. However, it is only since Vatican II that the modern understanding of the religious professional as described in this context has been appropriated by Roman Catholic priests. As I will argue in the conclusion, however, the process by which modern professions produce and legitimate professional or "official" knowledge—i.e., expert elites holding a monopoly on official knowledge—has an affinity with the way in which theological knowledge has traditionally been produced and legitimated within the Roman Catholic structure.

6. Haring notes, for example, that the notion of "invincible ignorance" has its origins in the noted seventeenth-century Catholic moralist St. Alphonsus Liguori.

7. It is not my purpose to go into detail about all the medical history of the AIDS epidemic or the social responses to the disease. Several other sources provide excellent information in this regard. Among these sources are Johnson and Vieira's (1987) discussion of etiology, Liebowitch's (1985) medical account of the discovery of the AIDS virus, and Shilts's (1987) journalistic treatment of the history of AIDS. Shilts, however, has been criticized for factual inaccuracies in his work.

8. *Bondings* is a publication of New Ways Ministries—an organization for gay Catholics that dissents from the church's official teaching on homosexuality.

9. Rusack died shortly after the AIDS Interfaith Council was formed. His position on the council was then filled by Oliver Garver, then the Suffragan Bishop of the Episcopal Diocese of Los Angeles.

10. For a fuller discussion of this letter and responses to it, see chapter 3.

Chapter 2. Methods

1. The following is the list of groups that indicated a normative response to the AIDS crisis: American Lutheran Church, Assemblies of God, Baptist General Conference, Christian Church (Disciples of Christ), Church of Jesus Christ of Latter-Day Saints, Church of Christ Scientist, Church of the Brethren, Church of the Foursquare Gospel, Church of the

Nazarene, Episcopal Church, Friends General Conference, Greek Ortho-
dox Archdiocese of North and South America, Jehovah's Witnesses,
Lutheran Church in America, Lutheran Church–Missouri Synod, National
Assembly of Bahais of the United States, Plymouth Brethren, Reformed
Church in America, Salvation Army, Seventh-Day Adventists, United
Church of Christ, United Methodist Church.

The following groups responded to a letter of inquiry but indicated
no response to the AIDS crisis: Buddhist Churches of America, Congregational Christian Churches, Conservative Baptist Association of America,
Islamic Center, Reorganized Church of Jesus Christ of Latter-Day Saints,
Southern Baptist Convention.

2. Articles were taken from the following publications: *Blueprint for
Social Justice* 39 (10) 1986; *Bondings* (Winter) 1985–86, (Winter)
1986–87; *Catholic Twin Circle*, 22 March 1987; *Charisma* (September)
1987; *Christianity and Crisis*, 24 June 1985, 13 January 1986, 19 May
1986, 2 March 1987; *The Christian Century*, 11–18 September 1985, 16
October 1985, 6–13 January 1988, 27 January 1988; *Christian Herald*
(January) 1988; *The Christian Ministry* (January) 1986; *Christianity
Today*, 18 October 1985, November 1985, 7 March 1986; *Commonweal*,
12 July 1985; *Liberty Report* (April) 1987; *Jewish Action* (Winter)
1986–87; *The Jewish Monthly* (April) 1987; *The Journal of Halacha and
Contemporary Society* 1987; *Journal of Pastoral Care* 41 (1) 1987; *Journal of Pastoral Counseling* 22 (1) 1987; *Journal of Psychology and Christianity* 6 (3) 1987; *St. Anthony's Messenger* (March) 1987; *Sojourners*
(February) 1986; *The United Church Observer* (January) 1988; *The Witness* (March) 1988. Entire issues of the following were devoted to articles
on AIDS or AIDS and homosexuality: *America* 156 (24) 1986, 158 (24)
1988; *Fidelity* 6 (10) 1987; *Engage/Social Action*, February 1986.

3. An organization of gay and lesbian Catholics.

4. In this public context Bishop Arzube stepped out of his role as
teacher and into a more pastoral role negotiating the church's official
teaching. This idea is discussed more fully in chapters 3 and 5.

5. Bohne notes that while these respondents claim to be "neutral,"
they harbor homophobic feelings.

Chapter 3. The Hierarchy Responds to AIDS

1. Reverend John Harvey (1987) expands on the Vatican position by
stating that homosexual sex is unhealthy even apart from AIDS. He cites
various diseases that may be contracted from homosexual sex. He also
notes that, theologically, homosexuality violates the procreative purpose

of human sexuality. AIDS is simply a further medical legitimation of the church's teaching

2. This statement was met with a great deal of opposition, not only from gay Catholics, but even among some bishops. Further, the United States Conference of Major Superiors of Men responded with a letter that stated in part that the Vatican statement "complicates our already complex ministry to all people." They continued: "Moreover, we find the arguments . . . are out of touch with modern psychological and sociological understandings of human sexuality."

3. Statements from other bishops and bishops' conferences in the United States include Bernardin 1986; Hickey 1987; New Jersey Catholic Conference 1987; Pennsylvania Conference on Interchurch Cooperation 1987; Pilla 1986; F. Quinn 1986; and J. Quinn 1986.

4. The California bishops issued an earlier statement on AIDS in 1986, but this dealt primarily with their opposition to a California ballot initiative (Proposition 64) to quarantine PWAs.

5. This position is similar to that found later in the document: "Abstinence outside and fidelity within marriage as well as the avoidance of intravenous drug abuse are the only morally correct and medically sure ways to prevent the spread of AIDS" (486). Monogamy per se is not advocated, but marital monogamy. The bishops allege that this is a medical as well as a moral recommendation.

6. Archbishop John L. May, president of the NCCB, appointed Mahony to head a redrafting committee for the statement. The committee was appointed to clarify any confusion over the church's teaching posed by the discussion of prophylactic AIDS education.

7. The bishops go on to cite their pastoral recommendations for homosexual persons: they should live chaste (that is, celibate) lives and develop loving relationships with persons of both sexes (see National Conference of Catholic Bishops 1973).

Chapter 4. Priests and AIDS Education

1. See Curran (1987, 274ff.) for a discussion of why sexual issues in particular have caused controversy in the church.

Chapter 5. Priest and PWAs

1. This division of labor is not absolute. While the bulk of a bishop's time is spent in official teaching, public appearances, ritual events,

administrative work, etc., he also has occasion to counsel and minister on the individual level. Often this includes counseling his priests. Conversely, priests, who spend a great deal of time ministering to individuals, also are public teachers of the church's doctrine, primarily when they preach at mass—the central public occasion of parish life.

2. This basis of authority is more akin to Weber's (1947) bureaucratic legitimation than to the charismatic type, in which access to the sacred is mediated through a particular individual.

3. While this counseling model has become dominant in Roman Catholicism only since Vatican II, Carroll (1981) and Long (1981) both note its emergence in nineteenth-century Protestantism.

4. These roles might have application more generally to priests' ministry to gay men and lesbians. In the Archdiocese of Los Angeles certain parishes have focused on ministry to gay and lesbian people and have attempted to "integrate" them into the life of the parish. However, these parishes still officially uphold the teaching of the church on sexual issues.

5. Beckley and Chalfant (1988) note that a great deal of research has indicated the importance of the clergyperson as counselor of first choice. They note that this is an important role for clergy in AIDS ministry. Yet they do not address the alienation PWAs may experience from the church because of their sexual orientation and the way this may alter PWAs' perception of clergy. Veroff, Kulka, and Douvan (1981), whom Beckley and Chalfant cite, note that Catholics and Fundamentalists seek priestly counsel more than other religious groups seek their clergy. Yet they also note that disaffiliated persons seek other sources for counseling. Beckley and Chalfant do not note this nuance.

Chapter 6. Toward an Analysis of Ecclesiastical Organization

1. Foucault's use of the concept of episteme is similar to Kuhn's (1970) use of the concept of a paradigm, in that both concepts involve the ways in which knowledge is created as well as the knowledge itself. Both theorists note that such systems of thought change over time. Kuhn calls such changes "paradigmatic shifts"; Foucault calls them "epistemic breaks in discourse." While the concepts of a shift in paradigm or an epistemic break have a heuristic value, they must be understood as historical fictions. Foucault, for example, uses the year 1656 as the landmark of when an epistemic shift occurred regarding the confinement of madness and a benchmark for the triumph of the Age of Reason (see Foucault 1965, 39). Such shifts in cultural understanding, of course, appear over

time and are prepared for by the slow evolution of events and become rei-fied in social consciousness only over time.

2. Cheney (1991, 179) notes a similar phenomenon with regard to organizational rhetoric. He writes: "Organizations, as rhetors, exploit the resource of ambiguity to manage multiple interests and multiple identities."

Chapter 7. Toward a Normative Critique of Church Structures

1. In the tradition of Catholic moral theology, a probable position is one for which a defensible theological case could be made, and over which theological dispute exists.

2. Kung (1988, 123–69) notes, for example, a whole progression not only of church teaching, but of paradigms through which church structure has moved in the past. At the same time, it is important to note that these movements, for the large part, are shifts in intellectual discourse, and lit-tle attention is given to the participation of subjugated discourses in the development of ecclesiastical discourse over time.

3. See also Congar's earlier work (1967, 314ff.) in which he raises the notion of reception. Congar sees the church as a living and developing reality. Congar gives a special place, in the development of teaching, to the magisterium, but also notes that the laity has a place in the development of church teaching. Yet in this earlier work reception carries more of a note of accepting, preserving, and transmitting church teaching. Congar is not clear, however, as to what role the laity might have in the transfor-mation of Church teaching as part of their activity of receiving.

4. In this context Mahoney (1987, 223) discusses the importance of the individual Christian as a moral subject and not simply the passive recipient of church teaching: "This [Christian personal experience] is the unique contribution of the participant rather than the spectator, the voy-ager and the eye-witness rather than the armchair traveller, the one who 'speaks from experience', and with the authority of a direct, immediate connection with events." While Mahoney does not see this experience as the only source of authority in the church, he sees it as an essential aspect of the way in which the Spirit teaches the church.

5. Paul VI is clearly echoing Pius XI's encyclical "Casti Connubi" (31 December 1930).

6. These authors present an in-depth discussion of the response to *Humanae Vitae* in the United States (92ff.).

REFERENCES

Abbott, Walter M., ed. 1966. *The documents of Vatican II*. American Press.

AIDS [special issue] 1986. *America* (June 28).

AIDS Interfaith Council. 1986. "Pastoral letter on our responsibility as religious leaders in the AIDS crisis and our response to Proposition 64, the LaRouche Initiative." AIDS Interfaith Council of Southern California, photocopy.

Albert, Edward. 1986 Acquired immune deficiency syndrome: the victim and the press. *Studies in Communication* 3:133–58.

Altman, Dennis. 1987. *AIDS in the mind of America*. Garden City, N.Y.: Anchor Press.

Antonio, Gene. 1986. *The AIDS cover-up?* San Francisco: Ignatius.

Bartholomew, John Niles. 1981. A sociological view of authority in religious organizations. *Review of Religious Research* 23:118–32.

Bayer, Ronald. 1985. AIDS and the gay community: Between the specter and the promise of medicine. *Social Research* 52:581–606.

Becker, Howard S., and Blanche Geer. 1957. Participant observation and interviewing: A comparison. *Human Organization*. 16 (3):28–32.

Beckley, Robert E., and H. Paul Chalfant. 1988. AIDS and pastoral counseling. Paper presented at the annual meeting of the Society for the Scientific Study of Religion and the Religious Research Association, 28 October.

Bennett, F. J. 1987. AIDS as a social phenomenon. *Social Science and Medicine* 25:529–39.

Benson, J. Kenneth, and James H. Dorsett. 1971. Toward a theory of religious organizations. *Journal for the Scientific Study of Religion* 10:138–51.

151

Berger, Joseph, Susan J. Rosenholtz, and Morris Zelditch, Jr. 1980. Status organizing processes. *Annual Review of Sociology* 6:479–508.

Berger, Peter L., and Thomas Luckman. 1967. *The sacred canopy*. Garden City, N.Y.: Doubleday.

Bernardin, Joseph. 1986. Pastoral letter on AIDS. *Origins* 16:383.

Biernacki, Patrick, and Dan Waldorf. 1981. Snowball sampling: Problems and techniques of chain referral sampling. *Sociological Methods and Research* 10:141–63.

Blau, Peter M., and Richard A. Schoenherr. 1971. *The structure of organizations*. New York: Basic.

Blush, Trudy Bloser. 1985. Challenging consciences. *Christian Century*, 6 March, 246–47.

Bocock, Robert. 1986. *Hegemony*. New York: Tavistock.

Boff, Leonardo. 1985. *Church, charism, and power*. New York: Crossroad.

Bohne, John. 1986. AIDS ministry issues for chaplains. *Pastoral Psychology* 34: 173–92.

Bottomore, Tom, Laurence Harris, V. G. Kiernan, and Ralph Miliband. 1983. *Dictionary of Marxist thought*. Cambridge: Harvard University.

Boyens, Sherrie. 1988. More than an epidemic. *Response* 20 (2): 22–23, 27.

Brandt, Allan M. 1987. *No magic bullet: A social history of venereal disease in the United States since 1880*. Expanded ed. New York: Oxford.

Briggs, Charles L. 1986. *Learning how to ask*. New York: Cambridge.

Burchard, Waldo W. 1954. Role conflicts of military chaplains. *American Sociological Review* 19:528–35.

Cahill, Lisa Sowle. 1987. Catholic sexual teaching: Context, function, and authority. In *Vatican authority and American Catholic dissent*, ed. William W. May, 187–205. New York: Crossroad.

California Catholic Conference. 1987. A call to compassion: A pastoral letter on AIDS. *Origins* 16:785, 787–90.

————. 1988. Principles and guidelines for the development of public policy regarding AIDS/ARC. Proposal, 14 January.

Callero, Peter. 1986. Toward a Meadian conception of role. *Sociological Quarterly* 27:343–58.

Carroll, Jackson W. 1981. Some issues in clergy authority. *Review of Religious Research* 23:99–117.

Castro, Michael R. 1987. *AIDS and the ministry of the church*. Nashville, Tenn: Discipleship Resources.

Charmaz, Kathy. 1981. The grounded theory method: An explication and interpretation. In *Contemporary field research*, ed. Robert M. Emerson, 109–26. Boston: Little, Brown.

Cheney, George. 1991. *Rhetoric in an organizational society: Managing multiple identities*. Columbia: University of South Carolina.

Cicourel, Aaron V. 1982. Interviews, surveys, and the problem of ecological validity. *American Sociologist* 17:11–20.

Congar, Yves. 1967. *Tradition and traditions*. Trans. Michael Naseby and Thomas Rainborough. New York: Macmillan.

———. 1972. Reception as an ecclesialogical reality. Trans. John Griffiths. *Concilium* 77:43–68.

Coser, Rose Laub. 1979. *Training in ambiguity*. New York: Free Press.

Curran, Charles E. 1982. *Moral theology: A continuing journey*. Notre Dame, Ind.: University of Notre Dame.

———. 1984. *Critical concerns in moral theology*. Notre Dame, Ind.: University of Notre Dame.

———. 1987. Destructive tensions in moral theology. In *The church in anguish*, ed. Hans Kung and Leonard Swidler, 273–78. San Francisco: Harper & Row.

Deedy, John. 1987. *American Catholicism: And now where?* New York: Plenum.

Denzin, N. K. 1970. *The research act in sociology*. London: Butterworth.

Dewey, Gerald. 1971. The resolution of role conflict among clergymen. *Sociological Analysis* 32:21–30.

Dingwall, Robert, and Phil M. Strong. 1985. The interactional study of organizations: A critique and reformulation. *Urban Life* 14:205–31.

Dionne, J. Robert. 1987. *The papacy and the church*. New York: Philosophical Library.

Dulles, Avery. 1978. *Models of the church*. New York: Doubleday.

Ebaugh, Helen Rose Fuchs. 1977. *Out of the cloister*. Austin: University of Texas.

Ellis, John Tracy. 1969. *American Catholicism*. Chicago: University of Chicago Press.

Episcopal Church General Convention. 1986. Resolution on AIDS. In *A time for caring*, ed. Lynne M. Coggi. New York: Episcopal Church Center.

The Ethical response to AIDS [special issue]. 1988. *America* (February 13).

Etzioni, Amitai. 1961. *A comparative analysis of complex organizations*. Glencoe, Ill.: Free Press.

Falwell, Jerry. 1987. AIDS: The judgement of God. *Liberty Report*, April, 2, 5.

Farley, Margaret A. 1987. Moral discourse in the public arena. In *Vatican authority and American Catholic dissent*, ed. William W. May, 168–86. New York: Crossroad.

Fichter, Joseph H. 1954. *Social relations in the urban parish*. Chicago: University of Chicago Press.

————. 1968. *America's forgotten priests: What are they saying*. New York: Harper & Row.

————. 1974. *Organization man in the church*. Cambridge, Mass.: Schneckman.

Fielding, Nigel G., and Jane L. Fielding. 1986. *Linking data*. Qualitative Methods Series 4. Newbury Park, Calif.: Sage.

Fischer, James A. 1987. *Priests: Images, ideals, and changing roles*. New York: Dodd, Mead.

Flynn, Eileen P. 1985. *AIDS: A Catholic call for compassion*. Kansas City, Mo.: Sheed & Ward.

Fortunato, John E. 1987. *AIDS: The spiritual dilemma*. San Francisco: Harper & Row.

Foucault, Michel. 1965. *Madness and civilization*. New York: Vintage.

————. 1973. *The order of things*. New York: Random House.

————. 1977. *Discipline and punish*. Trans. Alan Sheridan. New York: Pantheon.

———. 1980a. *The history of sexuality*. New York: Vintage.

———. 1980b. *Power and knowledge*. Ed. Colin Gordon. New York: Pantheon.

Frame, Randy. 1985. The church's response to AIDS. *Christianity Today*, 22 November, 50–51.

French, John R., Jr., and Bertram Raven. 1959. The bases of social power. In *Studies in social power*, ed. Dorwin Cartwright. Ann Arbor: University of Michigan.

Friedland, G. H., and R. R. Klien. 1987. Transmission of the human immunodeficiency virus. *New England Journal of Medicine* 317: 1125–35.

Friedson, Eliot. 1986. *Professional power*. Chicago: University of Chicago Press.

Gallup, George, Jr., and Jim Castelli. 1987. *The American Catholic people*. Garden City, N.Y.: Doubleday.

Geany, Dennis, and John Ring. 1971. *What a modern Catholic believes about priesthood*. Chicago: Thomas Moore.

Getzel, J. W., and E. G. Guba. 1954. Role, role conflict and effectiveness: An empirical study. *American Sociological Review* 19:164–175.

Glaser, Barney G., and Anselm Strauss. 1967. *The discovery of grounded theory*. New York: Aldine.

Gleason, Philip. 1979. In search of unity. *The Catholic Historical Review* 65:185–205.

Goffman, Erving. 1959. *The presentation of self in everyday life*. Garden City, N.Y.: Doubleday.

Goodwin, Ronald S. 1983. AIDS: A moral and political time bomb. *Moral Majority Report*, July, 2, 8.

Gordon, Kevin. 1986. Religion, moralizing, and AIDS. In *Homosexuality and Social Justice*, ed. Task Force on Gay and Lesbian Issues. San Francisco: The Consultation on Homosexuality, Social Justice, and Roman Catholic Theology.

Gramsci, Antonio. 1971. *Selections from the prison notebooks*. Ed. Quintin Hoare and Geoffrey Nowell Smith. London: Laurence & Wishart.

Gustafson, James M. 1961. *Treasure in earthen vessels*. Chicago: University of Chicago Press.

Hale, John P. 1988. The bishops' blunder. *America* 158:156–158, 171.

Hall, Douglass T., and Benjamin Schneider. 1973. *Organizational climates and careers*. New York: Seminar Press.

Hancock, Lee. 1985. Fear and healing in the AIDS crisis. *Christianity and Crisis* (June 24).

Haring, Bernard. 1970. A theological evaluation. In *The morality of abortion*, ed. John T. Noonan, Jr., 123–45. Cambridge: Harvard University.

Harris, C. C. 1969. Reform in a normative organization. *Sociological Review* 17:167–85.

Harrison, Beverly Wildung. 1985. *Making the connections*. Ed. Carol S. Robb. Boston: Beacon.

Hart, Roderick P. 1973. On applying Toulmin: The analysis of practical discourse. In *Explorations in rhetorical criticism*, ed. G. P. Mohrmann, Charles J. Stewart, and Donovan J. Ochs, 75–95. University Park: Pennsylvania State University.

Harvey, John F. 1987. *The homosexual person*. San Francisco: Ignatius.

Hebblethwaite, Peter. 1983. The popes and politics: Shifting patterns in "Catholic social doctrine." In *Religion and America*, ed. Mary Douglas and Steven Tipton, 190–206. Boston: Beacon.

Hewitt, J. P. 1979. *Self and society*. 2d ed. Boston: Allyn & Bacon.

Hickey, James. 1987. Most important is how he served. *Origins* 16:801, 803–4.

Holmes, Urban T., III. 1971. *The future shape of ministry*. New York: Seabury.

Horejsi, Gloria A. 1987. Support of AIDS staff. *Health and Social Worker* 12:229.

Horrigan, Alice. 1988. AIDS and the Catholic church. In *The social impact of AIDS in the United States*, ed. Richard A. Berk, 83–113. Cambridge, Mass.: Abt Books.

Hughes, Everett C. 1945. Dilemmas and contradictions of status. *American Journal of Sociology* 50:353–59.

———. 1971. *The sociological eye*. Chicago: Aldine.

John Paul II. 1981. *On the family (Familiaris consortio)*. Washington, D.C.: U.S. Catholic Conference.

Johnson, Edward S., and Jeffrey Vieira. 1986. Causes of AIDS: Etiology. In *AIDS: Facts and issues*, ed. Victor Gong and Norman Rudnick, 25–33. New Brunswick, N.J.: Rutgers.

Kennedy, Eugene C. 1988. *Tomorrow's Catholics, yesterday's church: The two cultures of American Catholicism.* New York: Harper & Row.

Kim, Gertrude. 1980. Roman Catholic organization since Vatican II. In *American denominational organization*, ed. Ross P. Sherer. Pasadena, Calif.: William Carey Library.

King, Geoffrey. 1977. The acceptance of law by the community. *Jurist* 37:233–65.

Kowalewski, Mark R. 1988. Double stigma and boundary maintenance. *Journal of Contemporary Ethnography* 17:211–228.

———. 1990. Religious responses to the AIDS crisis. *Sociological Analysis* 51:91–94.

Krauthammer, Charles. 1983. The politics of a plague. *The New Republic*, August, 18–21.

Kuhn, Thomas S. 1970. *The structure of scientific revolutions.* 2d ed. Chicago. University of Chicago Press.

Kung, Hans, and Leonard Swidler. 1987. *The church in anguish* New York: Harper & Row.

Kung, Hans. 1988. *Theology for the third millenium.* Trans. Peter Heinegg. New York: Doubleday.

Leibowitch, Jacques. 1985. *A strange virus of unknown origin.* Trans. Richard Howard. New York: Ballantine.

Lernoux, Penny. 1989. *People of God.* New York: Viking.

Long, Theodore E. 1981. Religion and therapeutic action: From healing power to medical magic. In *Religion and religiosity in America*, ed. Jeffrey K. Hadden and Theodore E. Long, 144–56. New York: Crossroads.

Lyng, Stephen G., and Lester Kurtz. 1985. Bureaucratic insurgency: The Vatican and the crisis of modernism. *Social Forces* 63:901–22.

Maduro, Otto. 1982. *Religion and social conflicts.* Trans. Robert R. Barr. Maryknoll, N.Y.: Orbis.

Magenau, John M., and Dean G. Pruitt. 1979. The social psychology of bargaining. In *Industrial relations*, ed. Geoffrey M. Stephanson and Christopher J. Brotherton, 181–210. New York: Wiley.

Mahoney, John. 1987. *The making of Moral Theology.* New York: Oxford University Press.

McKenzie, John. 1966. *Authority in the church.* New York: Sheed & Ward.

McNeill, John T. 1951. *A history of the cure of souls.* New York: Harper.

McSweeney, William. 1980. *Roman Catholicism: The search for relevance.* New York: St. Martin's.

Mead, George H. 1934. *Mind, self and society.* Chicago: University of Chicago Press.

Merton, Robert K. 1957. The role set: Problems in sociological theory. *British Journal of Sociology* 8:106–20.

Merton, Robert K., and Elinor Barber. 1976. *Sociological ambivalence.* New York: Free Press.

Metz, Johann Baptist. 1980. *Faith in history and society.* New York: Seabury.

Mieth, Dietmar. 1987. Moral doctrine at the cost of morality? In *The church in anguish*, ed. Hans Kung and Leonard Swidler, 125–43. San Francisco: Harper & Row.

Morin, Stephen F., and Walter F. Batchelor. 1984. Responding to the psychological crisis of AIDS. *Public Health Reports* 99:4–9.

National Conference of Catholic Bishops. 1976. *To live in Christ Jesus: A pastoral reflection on the moral life.* Washington, D.C.: U.S. Catholic Conference.

———. 1989. *Called to compassion and responsibility: A response to the HIV/AIDS crisis.* Washington, D.C.: U. S. Catholic Conference.

National Conference of Catholic Bishops, Committee on Pastoral Research and Practices. 1973. *Principles to guide confessors in questions of homosexuality.* Washington, D.C.: U.S. Catholic Conference.

National Council of Churches of Christ. 1986. Resolution on the churches' response to the AIDS crisis. Resolution adopted by the governing board, 22 May.

Nelson, James B. 1986. Responding to, learning from AIDS. *Christianity and Crisis* 46:176–81.

New Jersey Catholic Conference. 1987. Policy statement on AIDS. *Origins* 17:101,103–4.

Niebuhr, H. Richard. 1975. *Christ and culture.* New York: Harper & Row.

Nieckarz, Jim. 1985. Our fragile brothers. *Commonweal* 112:404–6.

O'Neill, David P. 1968. *The priest in crisis*. Dayton, Ohio: Pflaum.

Parsons, Talcott. 1952. *The social system*. London: Tavistock.

Patton, Cindi. 1986. *Sex and germs*. Boston: South End.

Paul VI. 1968. *On the regulation of birth (Humanae Vitae)*. New York: Paulist.

Pawell, Robert. 1986. AIDS: Crisis and compassion. *Blueprint for Social Justice* 39 (10): 1–7.

Pennsylvania Conference on Interchurch Cooperation. 1987. An interchurch statement on AIDS. *Origins* 17:180.

Pilla, Anthony. 1986. Addressing some underlying issues. *Origins* 16:692–96.

Plantinga, Cornelius, Jr. 1985. The justification of Rock Hudson. *Christianity Today*, 18 October, 16–17.

Presbyterian Church U.S.A. 1988. To meet AIDS with grace and truth. Resolution of the general assembly, St. Louis.

Pruitt, Dean G., and D. Leasel Smith. 1981. Impression management in bargaining: Images of firmness and trustworthiness. In *Impression management theory and social psychological research*, ed. James T. Tedeschi, 247–67. New York: Academic Press.

Quinn, Francis. 1986. Pastoral letter on AIDS. *Origins* 16:224.

Quinn, John R. 1986. The AIDS crisis: A pastoral response. *America*, 28 June, 504–6.

Reynaud, Jean-Daniel. 1988. Les regulations dans les organisations: Regulation de controle et regulation automnome. *Revue Francaise de Sociologie* 29:5–18.

Richardson, Jean L., Thomas Lochner, Kimberly McGuigan, and Alexandra M. Levine. 1987. Physician attitudes and experience regarding the care of patients with acquired immunodeficiency syndrome (AIDS) and related disorders. *Medical Care* 25:675–685.

Richardson, Kenneth D., and Robert B. Cialdini. 1981. Basking and blasting: Tactics of indirect self-presentation. In *Impression management theory and social psychological research*, ed. James T. Tedeschi, 41–53. New York: Academic Press.

Rossi, Peter H. 1988. On sociological data. In *Handbook of sociology*, ed. Neil J. Smelser, 131–54. Newbury Park, Calif.: Sage.

Sacred Congregation for the Doctrine of the Faith. 1986. *Letter to the bishops of the Catholic church on the pastoral care of homosexual persons*. Washington, D.C.: U.S. Catholic Conference.

———. 1992. Observations regarding legislative proposals concerning discrimination toward homosexual persons. *Origins* 22:175–177.

San Francisco welcomes the pope. 1987. *Fidelity* (October).

Sarbin, Theodore R., and Vernon L. Allen. 1968. Role theory. In *The handbook of social psychology*, ed. Gardner Lindzey and Elliot Aronson, 488–567. Reading, Mass.: Addison-Wesley.

Scherer, Ross P. 1980. The sociology of denominational organization. In *American denominational organization*, ed. Ross P. Scherer, 1–27. Pasadena, Calif.: William Carey Library.

Schoenherr, Richard A., and Andrew M. Greeley. 1974. Role commitment processes and the American priesthood. *American Sociological Review* 39:407–26.

Seidler, John. 1979. Priest resignations in a lazy monopoly. *American Sociological Review* 44:763–83.

———. 1986. Contested accommodation: The Catholic church as a special case of social change. *Social Forces* 64:847–74.

Seidler, John, and Katherine Meyer. 1989. *Conflict and change in the Catholic church*. New Brunswick, N.J.: Rutgers.

Selznick, Philip. 1948. Foundations of the theory of organization. *American Sociological Review* 13:25–35.

———. 1966. *TVA and the grass roots*. New York: Harper & Row.

Shelp, Earl E., and Ronald H. Sunderland. 1985. AIDS and the church. *Christian Century* 102:797–800.

———. 1987a. *AIDS and the church*. Philadelphia: Westminster.

———. 1987b. *AIDS: A manual for pastoral care*. Philadelphia: Westminster.

Shelp, Earl E., Ronald H. Sunderland, and Peter W. A. Mansell. 1986. *AIDS: Personal stories in pastoral perspective*. New York: Pilgrim.

Shibutani, T. 1961. *Society and personality: An interactionist approach to social psychology*. Englewood Cliffs, N.J.: Prentice-Hall.

Shilts, Randy. 1987. *And the band played on*. New York: St. Martin's.

Sider, Ronald J. 1988. AIDS: An evangelical perspective. *Christian Century* 105:11–14.

Simmel, George. 1955. *Conflict and the web of group-affiliations*. New York: Free Press.

Special issue on AIDS. 1985–86. *Bondings* [special issue]. (Winter).

Special issue on AIDS. 1986–87. *Bondings* [special issue]. (Winter).

Stone, Cathy. 1986. When others care. *Disciple*, November, 19–21.

Strauss, Anselm, and Juliet Corbin. 1990. *Basics of qualitative research*. Newbury Park, Calif.: Sage.

Struzzo, John A. 1970. Professionalism and the resolution of authority conflicts among the Catholic clergy. *Sociological Analysis* 31:92–106.

Sweeney, Terrance A. 1992. *A church divided: The Vatican versus American Catholics*. Buffalo, N.Y.: Prometheus.

Tedeschi, James T., and Marc Reiss. 1981. Identities, the phenomenal self, and laboratory research. In *Impression management theory and social psychological research*, ed. James T. Tedeschi, 3–22. New York: Academic Press.

Thoits, Peggy A. 1987. Negotiating roles. In *Spouse, parent, worker*, ed. Faye J. Crosby, 11–22. New Haven: Yale University Press.

Thompson, Victor. 1966. *Modern Organizations*. New York: Alfred A. Knopf.

Troelstch, Ernst. 1981. *The social teaching of the Christian churches*. Trans. Olive Wyon. Chicago: University of Chicago Press.

Trow, Martin. 1957. Comment on "Participant observation and interviewing: A comparison." *Human Organization* 16:33–35.

Turner, Ralph H. 1956. Role-taking, role standpoint, and reference-group behavior. *American Journal of Sociology* 61:316–28.

United Church of Christ. 1987. Proposed pronouncement on health and wholeness in the midst of a pandemic. Statement endorsed at the General Synod of the United Church of Christ, June.

United Methodist Church, General Board of Discipleship. 1986. Resolution on ministry in the midst of the AIDS epidemic. Resolution adopted on 28 February.

United States Catholic Conference of Bishops. 1983. *The challenge of peace: God's promise and our response*. Washington, D.C.: U.S. Catholic Conference.

———. 1985. *Economic justice for all: Catholic social teaching and the U.S. economy*. Washington, D.C.: U.S. Catholic Conference.

U.S. Catholic Conference of Bishops Administrative Board. 1987. The many faces of AIDS: A gospel response. *Origins* 17:481, 483–93.

Vaillancourt, Jean-Guy. 1980. *Papal power*. Berkeley: University of California.

Varacalli, Joseph A. 1983. *Toward the establishment of liberal Catholicism in America*. Washington, D.C.: University Press of America.

Vaux, Kenneth. 1985. AIDS as crisis and opportunity. *Christian Century* 102:910–11.

Veroff, Joseph, Richard A. Kulka, and Elizabeth Douvan. 1981. *Mental health in America*. New York: Basic Books.

Weber, Max. 1947. *The theory of social and economic organizations*. Trans. A. M. Henderson and Talcott Parsons. New York: Free Press.

Welch, Sharon. 1985. *Communities of resistance and solidarity*. New York: Orbis.

Whyte, William F. 1956. *The organization man*. New York: Simon & Schuster.

Wilding, Paul. 1982. *Professional power and social welfare*. London: Routledge & Kegan Paul.

Windsor, Pat. 1987. AIDS: How should the church respond. *St. Anthony Messenger*, March, 21–27.

Winter, Gibson. 1968. *Religious identity: A study of religious organization*. New York: Macmillan.

Wolf, James G. 1987. Homosexuality and religious ideology: Gay Catholic priests in the United States. Paper presented at the annual meeting of the American Sociological Association, August.

Woods, Richard. 1985. AIDS, not a gay disease, the black death of our era. *National Catholic Reporter*, 6 September. Reprinted in *Bondings* (1985 Winter): 3.

World Council of Churches of Christ. 1987. AIDS and the church as a healing community. Resolution approved by the central committee in Geneva, Switzerland, 24 January.

INDEX